TRIUMPH OF
JUSTICE

AN ORTHODOX JEWISH RABBI

THE TRIUMPH
OF JUSTICE

MorningStar Publications
A DIVISION OF MORNINGSTAR FELLOWSHIP CHURCH
375 Star Light Drive, Fort Mill, SC 29715

The Triumph of Justice
by An Orthodox Jewish Rabbi
Lev David Ministries
Copyright © 2008

Distributed by MorningStar Publications, Inc.,
a division of MorningStar Fellowship Church,
375 Star Light Drive, Fort Mill, SC 29715

MorningStar's website: www.MorningStarMinistries.org
For information call: 1-800-542-0278

International Standard Book Number—978-1-59933-435-6

Cover Design: Kevin Lepp
Book Layout: Pattie Hale

Unless otherwise indicated, all Scripture quotations are taken from the New American Standard Bible, copyright © 1960, 1962, 1963, 1968, 1971, 1973, 1974, 1977 by The Lockman Foundation. Italics in Scripture are for emphasis only.

TABLE OF CONTENTS

INTRODUCTION

JUSTICE IS A TOPIC THAT WE DO NOT WANT to hear about often in the church. It still amazes me to find myself writing a book on the subject, mostly because I was so badly hurt in the past by what has been labeled justice. I went to a Christian college where a great many of the professors ascribed to a social-justice gospel.[1] By the end of my four years there, I was personally so turned off to the topic or idea of justice that I wanted nothing to do with it. The guilt-manipulation and self-righteousness that I saw associated with justice there made me disgusted with the entire topic.

A good number of years now separate me from those experiences. What I have learned in the interim is that it was not justice that was the problem—it was me. I had been damaged and hurt, so I was in a sense lashing out at *a* truth of gospel, rather than seeking *the* truth of the gospel. It took me a number of years, and becoming a rabbi and even a Jewish judge, before I was completely healed and able to learn what justice was truly about.

---

1   The social justice gospel will be elucidated later in the book.

When I was first asked to write an article on justice for the church, I almost laughed because I thought few would want to read it. Much like Sarah, when she was told to prepare for the child of promise, I was not ready for what God had prepared, both in me and in the body of Christ. It seems that for some time the Lord has been preparing the hearts and minds of His people for a rebirth of godly justice within His body.

Justice is of vital importance to God. As there is consideration about the reestablishment of a system of justice within the church, it is vitally important to examine not only how justice is supposed to work, but also how it can be abused. When justice is abused, it is lost. The mistakes of others, if properly examined, can help keep us from making them ourselves. If justice is so vitally important to God that He would destroy so many, as well as His holy temple when it was violated, then we, too, need come with a holy fear into the place of judgment, careful not to make the same mistakes.

I truly believe that when the body of Christ gets this right, it will open unimaginable doors for the gospel to be spread throughout the world. A simple look at human history will demonstrate that there is a deep longing in the hearts of men for justice. The establishment of governments and the revolutionary overthrow of tyranny all has at its core, amongst other desires, a desire for justice. Whether it was the establishment of the democratic government of the United States or the communist government of the Soviet Union, each was an attempt by man to establish a system of justice upon the world. Each to a different extent was also infected with a degree of humanism and human logic, thus making even the best system man could create inherently flawed.

I would argue that God in His Word laid down, amongst a great number of other things, a system of justice that is truly righteous. By its very nature and origin, it is perfect and without flaw. This is not to say that the operation of such a system will be inerrant. It has been given into human hands, and thus its perfection in execution is limited by human understanding and imperfection. However, the foundational elements are heavenly. In Exodus 25:9, Moses is commanded, **"According to all that I am going to show you, as the pattern of the tabernacle and the pattern of all its furniture, just so you shall construct it."** The rabbis comment that this is an allusion to all of Scripture. It reflects a heavenly blueprint for all of life, spirituality, and government—essentially, as it is in heaven, so is it on earth.

The highest level of worship that we may experience here on earth will pale in comparison to the worship we will experience in heaven, yet we do not cease our worship. Likewise, even though the best system of justice that we may form on this earth will by far pale in comparison to the justice that the Lord Jesus Christ will establish at His return, this does not mean that we should cease from its establishment or its betterment. As long as we strive to purify our hearts and build upon a true foundation, it can only glorify His name.

Ultimately, justice must be built on the firm foundation of the true gospel of Christ. Paul states, **"And when I came to you, brethren, I did not come with superiority of speech or of wisdom, proclaiming to you the testimony of God. For I determined to know nothing among you except Jesus Christ, and Him crucified"** (**I Corinthians 2:1-2**). This is the only true foundation of the gospel, and it was the foundation for all of Paul's teaching. Even his own beautiful soliloquies on the topic of justice, by his own words here, had Christ and His atoning work as their foundation. If we hold firm to this foundation and build only on it, and if we make our every deed and all our efforts to show forth and proclaim the glory of it, then the reestablishment of justice within the body of Christ and the establishment of true justice throughout the world will succeed.

CHAPTER ONE
THE TRIAL OF JESUS—
HOW JUSTICE FAILED

THIS CHAPTER, LIKE MUCH OF THIS BOOK in general, was originally published as an article in *The Morning Star Journal*. At that time, Rick Joyner felt the need to add a comment beforehand as an encouragement to receive the material as it was intended. I agreed with everything that Rick said in that brief introduction and have not been able to find a better way to say it. Also, I believe that such an exhortation is better coming from someone who stands in the non-Jewish part of the body, than coming from me. Therefore, I have decided to include Rick's quote in its entirety here:

> *One of the most tragic mistakes made by Christians throughout the Middle Ages was to blame the Jews for the crucifixion of Jesus. Such thinking could not be more flawed—it was the Jewish people who gave us Jesus, the Bible, and the foundation of almost every good thing in Western civilization. They have certainly fulfilled the prophecy given to Abraham that his descendants would be a blessing to every family on the face of the earth. The Jewish people have also, in a most extraordinary way,*

helped give the world a system of justice that is the fairest that can be found on the earth.

The American government with its system of justice has been in existence for nearly two hundred fifty years. We have some brilliant and some very bad administrations, as well as courts. Even the best form of government will be a bad government if you have bad people in it. The Jewish system of justice has been on the earth for nearly four thousand years. You would have to expect them to likewise have had some bad courts along the way. This article highlights how one Jewish court violated many of its own basic rules to condemn Jesus.

Just as it would not be justice to judge all of American history by just one administration, it is likewise foolish to judge Jewish justice and history by one bad case, even if it was the most important case of all time. However, it was by this mistake that salvation came to the world. It was a mistake that God planned for and used to bless us all. Even though this trial has some remarkable and important lessons in it, let us by no means use it to blame the Jewish people through whom we have all been so blessed.

*~*Rick Joyner

Without doubt one of the lowest moments in the judiciary history of the Jewish people was the trial and execution of the Lord Jesus Christ. It is interesting to note that the Jewish people, possibly more than any other, see that justice is one of the core issues in the heart of God, and yet, in the most important trial of all time, some profound mistakes were made leading to the condemnation of the righteous.

They believed that the flood came upon the world because of the injustice of robbery running unchecked throughout the world. They also believed that the destruction suffered by Sodom and Gomorrah was the result of injustice toward strangers manifested in a cruel lack of hospitality. They believed that the first temple was destroyed not because of rampant idolatry, rather because of the injustice suffered by the widow, the orphan, and the needy in the society of that day. They believed that the second temple was destroyed because of baseless hatred which perverted justice for its own sake. So it is not such a stretch to see that with injustice rampant in Israel, basic mistakes were made with the trial of Jesus. However, as I think about this event, I am compelled to ask if that was all that was going on—if perhaps there is not more to the story than we first see.

Every court throughout history has had its guidelines of order on how it is run. These rules are often called the rules of court, and they govern who sits on the judiciary, how cases are heard, how evidence may be presented, who can present evidence when cases are heard, and so on. These rules may seem boring and taxing on our patience, especially as they are always (or at least supposed to be) followed. It is only when these rules are not followed that they begin to become at all interesting. When every rule that is set into place is completely disregarded in order to accuse and convict a person, then these rules become vitally important. Therefore, we will take a look at the rules of court that should have been involved in the days of Jesus, and then examine His trial—in this way we can see what went wrong.

The first rule that needs to be discussed is that of who may serve as judges. Beyond the long preparatory period, there were and continue to be in the Jewish system other requirements set forth for judges. People were not and are still not appointed as judges lightly. Being a judge among the people of Israel takes years of dedicated study, both in the general laws of Torah, but more so in the various aspects of justice and biblical morality. This is accompanied by a period of discipleship, which runs much like an apprenticeship for several years. The Talmud[2,3] states that there are three primary types of cases which require judges with different qualities. The first type of cases listed are monetary cases. These cases could be judged by anyone over the age of majority who had either been ordained a judge or had been accepted as a judge by the parties at hand.

The second type of cases are those that resulted in corporal punishment. The Jewish judiciary decided that the rules needed to be a little more stringent than those required of someone who only deals with money. Therefore, it was decided that to hear such cases a judge

---

2   The following information is taken in paraphrase form from the Tractate Sanhedrin starting on page 38A and proceeding through until about 57B.

3   The primary work of rabbinic commentary on the Bible—thus the source of all modern Jewish law.

had to be ordained by one who had been ordained before. An average citizen could not be accepted by the parties involved; rather a real judge was now needed. At this level, a priest, Levite, or common Israeli, whose daughters[4] would be eligible to marry a proper priest, were the only ones eligible to be judges.

Third, there were capital cases. Here the judges had even more stringent rules laid upon them, one of which was that priests and Levites could not serve as judges in capital cases. The reasoning for this rule was fairly simple: The rabbis did not want the court to easily hand down death sentences. Because the priests and Levites were the ones who performed the regular sacrifices in the temple, they did not trust them to be squeamish enough at the sight of blood and the thought of dying things to allow them to judge capital cases.

Also, the person who was to be a judge in a capital case was not allowed to be known as angry, mean, or cruel. Rather they wanted people who were renowned for their compassion and love of people. Essentially, with the bloodthirsty and sadistic eliminated, they wanted to find the most merciful and compassionate people they could and stack the court full of them to avoid the miscarriage of justice for the accused. Over the course of time, from Moses to Jesus, Judaism grew

---

4   The Bible lays down different rules dealing with things such as idolatry and the like that would disqualify one's progeny from marrying a proper priest.

and developed. The prophets, though often disregarded in their own lifetimes, had incredible influence upon the religion as a whole—how it viewed itself and the world around it. Primarily on account of the prophetic witness, Judaism morphed from a typical near-eastern religion, which had little respect for human life, into one with a genuine culture of life—to the point that it became a part of Jewish scriptural interpretation that any law except three, murder, idolatry and incest,[5] could be violated in order to save a life.[6] This culture of life carried over even into the Jewish justice system. It is written in the Talmud that if a court put two people to death within seventy years, they were a court of violence and blood.[7]

After determining who could be a judge, then there were rules for how cases were heard. Both monetary cases and cases that dealt with higher forms of punishment had to be started during the day, during fourth hour and before the ninth hour. The reason for this is that these were the times of prayer. In Jesus' time, people would rise before sunrise, immerse in a mikveh,[8] and then from one hour before sunrise until the fourth hour they would

---

5   The term "incest" biblically and in rabbinic literature, means any of a number of forbidden sexual relationships.
6   This in itself has incredible ramifications for much of the actions of Jesus, especially those in which He is accused of violating the Sabbath—sadly, time will fail me to elaborate upon that further.
7   Talmud Makkot 7A
8   A ritual bath or baptismal, which men partake of every day to cleanse themselves from spiritual impurity, was absolutely required for one wanting to enter the temple.

pray. It was very important to the rabbis that God be brought into the situation as much as possible.

Once started, monetary cases could, if necessary, be finished at night and on the same day that they were started. With corporal and capital cases, once started they could only be finished during the day, not at nighttime. They also could not be finished on the same day that they started; rather, it had to be at least a two-day process. The judges were supposed to sleep on their thoughts and decisions.

Cases could not be started on the Sabbath or on festivals, as these were days of Holy Convocation on which the people were required to be consumed with the worship of God, not these other matters. They also could not be started on the day before any of these days, as they were days of preparation. In other words, it was assumed that on the days before these holidays, the judges' minds would be preoccupied with preparation to the point that they might make errors in their judgment. Again, we are concerned with being careful not to pervert or distort justice.

With monetary cases, two witnesses were not always required. If the guilty party stated that he was guilty and wanted to repent, he was taken at his word, and the proper punishment was meted out. With higher cases, if the accused admitted his guilt, not only was his testimony not accepted, but except for a very few cases, the death penalty was immediately taken off the table; almost any form of repentance was enough to spare a person his life.

For the death penalty to be an option, there had to be two witnesses to the crime, and both had to try to prevent the accused from going forth with the crime, warning him that he would be liable to death if he fought off his two restrainers and managed to go forward with the sin in any case. In addition to all of this, the requirements we have discussed for witnesses were also in effect, such as the witnesses not being related to the accused, the plaintiff, or to each other. In capital and corporal cases, the witnesses could also not be judges, at least not those hearing the case, nor could the judges be related to the witnesses in any way or directly connected to them through financial matters.

Monetary cases could be overturned either from acquittal to conviction or from conviction to acquittal. Corporal and capital cases on the other hand could only be overturned in favor of acquittal. Not only were they willing to acquit, but up until the very second of execution for the punishment, if a new witness came forward with new evidence, then the entire case was reheard with all of the strictures that we discussed above.

So if a person was found guilty of a capital crime while he was being led to be executed and a new witness came forward and wanted their evidence heard, then the accused and the entire court was brought back and the case was reheard during at least a two-day trial. According to the rabbis, this could be done up to one thousand times in order to ensure that justice was served.

The procedure for this is actually rather interesting. They would leave one of the judges behind at the door to the Sanhedrin, and with him they would leave a flag. If a new witness came to present evidence, the person at the door would begin to wave the flag. Meanwhile, at the site of execution there would have been another judge whose sole job was to watch for the waving of the flag. This is an interesting image when compared to Acts 7:58, **"And the witnesses laid down their clothes at the feet of a young man named Saul"** (NKJV). The word translated here as **"clothes"** is actually better translated as flag. It would appear that it was at least possible that Saul, who later became Paul, was the very judge in the trial of Stephen and was left with the command to wave the flag if anyone new came to give evidence.

In monetary cases, the discussion and the voting among the judges could start with either the greatest or the least. However, when it came to cases of higher importance, the discussion and the voting started with the least and finished with the greatest. This was done so that the thoughts and decisions of the more learned and respected of the court would not inadvertently influence those of lesser learning and honor. Especially in courts that heard cases of higher importance such as capital cases, it was likely that both student and teacher would sit on the same court. It was a break of decorum for students to publicly contradict their teachers; therefore, it was decided that the lesser would make their arguments and decisions before the greater.

Finally, monetary cases could be decided by a majority of only one, and it goes without saying that a unanimous vote was also acceptable. In cases of higher importance, a majority of three was required; a simple majority was enough to acquit but not enough to convict. If only one or two wanted to convict as opposed to acquit, the case was reheard. If a similar decision was reached again, an acquittal was given. In the case of a unanimous vote, it held in corporal cases but was unacceptable in capital cases. In capital cases, a unanimous vote was counted as an acquittal that could not be overturned.

If all of this sounds like they did not want to put people to death, then you are understanding correctly. The question then becomes this: What went wrong with Jesus? Why was it so easy and quick to put Him to death? The answer to these questions, while vital for us to understand, is at the same time incredibly saddening. Jesus' death was more than anything a political play, an elimination of a political threat on many different levels couched in the language and trappings of a proper trial. Without doubt it was a miscarriage of justice that came about in order to fulfill someone's personal and political agenda.

The Trial of Jesus

We will now go through the trial and execution of the Lord Jesus Christ verse by verse and examine exactly what was not done, what was ignored, and then we will look at some of the reasons why these things could possibly have happened that way.

Starting in Luke, it says, **"Having arrested Him, they led Him and brought Him into the high priest's house. Now the men who held Jesus mocked Him and beat Him. And having blindfolded Him, they struck Him on the face" (see Luke 22:54, 63-64 NKJV).** There are several very glaring violations that we see in these early verses of the ordeal. The first is that the trial was being held at the home of the high priest and not at the Sanhedrin building which was inside the temple court.[9] Second, it seems the high priest was actually going to sit as judge for the case. Then there was the problem that the arrest and trial were being held at night. There was also the problem that the trial was being held on the first day of Passover, when in actuality, the entire month of Nissan, the Jewish month in which Passover occurs, is considered a festival month, and no trial can occur during that entire month. In fact, it is even forbidden to issue a summons to court while it is still the month

---

9   It is interesting to note that according to the Talmud, at the start of any festival, the Sanhedrin building was locked and guarded, and the head of the court (a judge qualified to hear capital cases) held the key, and only he could order the court opened again.

of Nissan, and required a person to appear after the month is over. Finally, we have the problem that Jesus was receiving corporal punishment without a trial. A slap across the face in itself would have enabled Him to push forward His own lawsuit and would have given reasonable grounds for Him to seek a dismissal of the one that He was now facing, against the rules.

Matthew goes on to state the following:

> Now the chief priests, the elders, and all the council[10] sought false testimony against Jesus to put Him to death,
>
> but found none. Even though many false witnesses came forward, they found none. But at last two false witnesses came forward
>
> and said, "This fellow said, 'I am able to destroy the temple of God and to build it in three days.'"
>
> And the high priest arose and said to Him, "Do You answer nothing? What is it these men testify against You?"
>
> But Jesus kept silent. And the high priest answered and said to Him, "I put You under oath by the living God: Tell us if You are the Christ, the Son of God" (Matthew 26:59-63 NKJV).

There are a great number of things that were happening which simply went against Jewish judicial

---

10   Note that neither Matthew nor Luke uses the word Sanhedrin. The absence in Luke's Gospel is the most glaring especially as he makes use of the term in Acts.

procedure. First, priests were seated on a court for a capital crime. Second, this court was actively seeking to put Jesus to death, when neutrality leaning toward acquittal was necessary. Third, the court allowed any number of false witnesses to come forward to try and put Jesus to death. This was a major problem because biblically a false witness was supposed to receive the punishment he was trying to lay on another. In other words, all of these false witnesses were supposed to be tried, most likely found guilty, and then put to death. Instead, the high priest, in his supposedly great zeal to see Scripture upheld, seemed to neglect some of the most important parts.

When they finally found two witnesses, all they could report was that supposedly Jesus had claimed He was able to tear down a building, albeit the temple, and rebuild it in three days. While talk of destroying the temple was, by rabbinical enactment, a blasphemy,[11] the violation of a rabbinical decree was typically only a fine, and at worst lashes. The death penalty should have been off the table at this point.

Next, the high priest bound Jesus with an oath. This, too, was very problematic. While in Judaism, we will at times bind people with oaths or make them swear oaths in our courts, it is only when they have actually said something. Finally, we never swear by the living God, but only on the Torah Scroll, and even then not as a

---

11 Jesus never Himself spoke of destroying the temple, so still He is free from even transgressing a rabbinical decree.

matter of course. If someone lies in such a vow, it forever disqualifies that person from being a witness. This is only done as an extreme measure when we believe that someone is so lacking in basic integrity that they would lie to get out of a spot, and even then we only make them swear as to the veracity of the statement that they have already made.

We have already discussed that a person could not give condemning evidence about themselves in a capital case. Therefore, the high priest, who was not even qualified to be hearing this case, could not make Jesus do so; furthermore, he certainly could not bind Him with a vow to do so. It was not the United States' Bill of Rights that came up with the idea of the Fifth Amendment (having the right to remain silent as your testimony might incriminate you); this was a thoroughly Jewish idea.

Matthew then continues with the account: **"Jesus said to him, 'It is as you said. Nevertheless, I say to you, hereafter you will see the Son of Man sitting at the right hand of the Power, and coming on the clouds of heaven.' Then the high priest tore his clothes, saying, 'He has spoken blasphemy! What further need do we have of witnesses? Look, now you have heard his blasphemy! What do you think?' They answered and said, 'He is deserving of death'"** (Matthew 26:64-66).

First, let me clarify what blasphemy is according to the Talmud.[12] Blasphemy that led to death, according

12 Sanhedrin 96A and Berachot 24B

24

to the rabbis of Jesus' time, was the cursing of God by God's own Name. In other words, let us say that Peloni is a name of God. To commit true blasphemy, which would actually cause a person to be killed, in the presence of two witnesses who had tried to stop and warn him of the punishment, he would say, "May Peloni curse Peloni." Then, just to make sure he had really meant to say it, he had to say it a second time in the presence of those two witnesses. To say, **"It is as you said,"** is not by any means blasphemy which leads to death—perhaps a fine or a beating, but not death.

I stop with the **"it is as you said"** piece because the rest of Jesus' words are Him quoting Targum Yonaton, which was an Aramaic translation/commentary of the Hebrew Bible, in this case from the Book of Daniel. Quoting Scripture, especially in the presence of the elders and priests is never a sin, so there could have been no blasphemy there.

The high priest's reaction was also problematic. One, the judges, as we discussed earlier, could not act as witnesses. Second, a person could never be baited into incidentally committing a capital offense, as was the high priest's intent here. Third, the high priest was forbidden from telling the people what they should think. Finally, an immediate verdict was demanded. Again, this was a problem. The verdict given on the same day, or in this case at night when the case began, violated more prohibitions and judicial rules.

The most telling part of this entire case, however, was yet to occur. In the very next chapter, they led Jesus to Pontius Pilate in order to be executed. At first you may think this made sense. The problem was that when the Sanhedrin, or at least a similar court, later decided to put Stephen to death,[13] they did not feel the need to go to the governor; rather they did the execution themselves. Judaism, especially within the province of Palestine, held the status of Religio Legatus, a legal religion under Roman law, which meant as long as they kept the Romans happy, they were free to dispose of their troublemakers as they saw fit. So why would they want to take this specific case to the Roman governor? The answer is interesting.

With the abounding number of courtroom dramas which seem to be inundating our culture in the United States of late, I doubt you would find many people who do not have a basic idea of how the court system works in the United States. Suppose you were told a story about the mayor of some town who had someone arrested, and then tried the person without benefit of a lawyer and jury. After the trial, he immediately took him to the chief of police, who promptly shot the person. You would probably think someone was telling you a bad piece of fiction, devoid of any of the facts.

---

13   A decision which may have had more to do with him being a Samaritan than actually violating the Torah.

When the first-century Jews read the Gospels, or most people to whom the Gospels originally went, they would have had a fairly good idea how a Jewish court system did and did not work. To them, this would either look like a bad piece of fiction or a serious political vendetta. As truth is often stranger than fiction, it is the latter.

The Gospel writers most likely wanted us to ask several questions: Where was Rabbi Gamaliel, who was the elegant voice of reason in the Book of Acts? (see Acts 5:34-39) It is understood from the Talmud and the historical records of the time that he, not the high priest, was head of the Sanhedrin at this time,[14] and as stated earlier, Saul, who would become Paul, was possibly one of the judges. Where were they?

It is known that Rabbi Gamaliel would extend his Passover Seder from the evening all the way to the time of prayer the next morning and that he would interrupt it for nothing. Then he would pray for the festival service, which according to the Talmud would take him five or six hours. This means that by the time Gamaliel even allowed the events of the outside world to enter his mind, it was already the fifth or sixth hour of the day, at which point

---

14 Historically, there is some debate as to when Jesus was born and thus when He would have died. Biblically, we know that He was tried at the age of 33. The earliest possible time scholars believe He could have been born was 8BCE, the latest being 4CE. This would range His death anywhere from 25CE to 37CE. Gamaliel ascended to the position of Nasi (head of the Sanhedrin) in the Jewish year of 3731, which equates to somewhere between 19 and 20BCE. It was a position held until death, and we know biblically that he was still alive after the execution of Jesus.

Jesus was already crucified (see Luke 23:44). By this time, there was little left that he could do.

Why would Caiaphas and Annas, the two high priests, want Pilate to kill Jesus? Several problems existed within Judean society at this time. First, the people were divided. The Sadducean sect, with the support of Rome, held control of the temple, while the Pharisaic sect, with the support of Rome, held control over the court system. The Romans desired to keep the people thus divided as it made them easier to rule and less likely to have a successful revolt.

Jesus was a threat to the Sadducean sect on account of being a descendant of David. The Sadducees were in fact the remnants of the Maccabees, priests who drove out the Greeks and set themselves up as both priests and kings. A possible Davidic heir with huge popular support was a threat to the political power for which the Sadducees were vying. However, they also saw the potential to make some headway against the Pharisees, who themselves held a huge sway over the people, if for no other reason than that they could actually try people and inflict punishments, including death. If the Sadducees could essentially have one of their enemies executed, at least in their minds they could gain the necessary political power to pull ahead of the Pharisees.

However, in doing this, they could not let the Pharisees know what was going on or they would likely mobilize to stop them. Josephus[15] records that this was actually the

---

15   Antiquities of the Jews 20:200

case with regard to Jesus' brother James. The Sadducees, then under the sole leadership of Annas, put James to death against the Pharisees' wishes (they actually counted James as one of their own) while the Roman governor was out of the area. Upon the governor's return, the Pharisees demanded retribution, and in an odd sort of God's justice, Annas, the high priest, was crucified on Golgotha just as he had done to Jesus. Even in this, there is a lesson concerning justice in the kingdom; God takes it very seriously, and if justice is perverted, consequences will be suffered.

Therefore, they took Jesus to the Roman governor and had Him crucified. Pontius Pilate seemingly played a rather innocent role in this, but there are some things that stick out. Historically, we know several things about Pilate.

First, he had been embarrassed on several occasions by the Jews when he had tried to erect Roman images within the temple, embarrassments from which he was still smarting in a very real way. Second, he had seen his fill of uprisings, upstart Messiahs, and Davidic kings, to the point where he was almost developing a rather severe paranoia, something that would eventually lead to his own execution back in Rome. Third and most important, he was sorely upset that he had never been able to get any of the Jews to swear allegiance to Rome or to Caesar—that is until now. **"And he said to the Jews, 'Behold your King!' But they cried out, 'Away with Him, away with Him! Crucify Him!' Pilate said to them, 'Shall I** crucify your King?' The chief priests answered, 'We have no king but Caesar!'" (see John 19:14-15 NKJV) Thus the death of Jesus was politically expedient for both parties. The Sadducees managed to get rid of what to them was a thorn in their side. They also managed to gain some political clout against the Pharisees. Meanwhile, Pilate got what he always wanted from the Jews. Instead of them responding, "We have no king but God," he finally got them to say, **"We have no king but Caesar,"** the very words of allegiance that he always desired to extract from his subjects.

It is vitally important to see how justice can be misused and perverted for the sake of political gain or the expedience of the moment. As we go forth in seeking Christian justice, there will always be the temptation for the elders to bend the rules just a little bit, to twist things just the smallest amount, in order to protect the things they hold dear—what they view as their own territory of influence they wish to guard, or even as a way of settling old scores. All of these things are possibilities for temptation.

Sadly, once justice has been perverted, there is no unperverting it. The damage has been done, lives have been damaged, and the glory of the Lord has been profaned. For this very reason, it is important to understand that it can happen, that it has happened, and that—God forbid—it could happen again. Out of those who did pervert justice, those who led the way in the case of Jesus; Pilate was recalled to Rome, divested of wealth, and beheaded for gross negligence of duties; Caiaphas, according to

Talmudic accounts, was later skinned alive by Pilate for inciting a riot; and Annas was crucified on the very hilltop where he had the Lord of glory killed.

The elders of the church are supposed to be the vehicle for God's justice within His body. However, if the church is truly seeking justice, and one of those elders decides to pervert it, God will grant the church its wish. God help that elder when He does, for God's justice is perfect; it is true and it repays measure for measure. Hence Jesus' warning in Matthew 7:2: **"For with what judgment you judge, you will be judged; and with the measure you use, it will be measured back to you"** (NKJV). If we truly want to judge God's kids, then let us do so with just and accurate judgment, seeking only the best for all involved and granting mercy whenever possible.

All of this is not to exonerate or completely acquit the elders of that time. That this happened on their watch makes them just as guilty as those who actually tried Jesus to put Him to death. Biblically, it is a basic principle that the elders, the judges, are held responsible for the spiritual state of their cities. It is even stated biblically that if a body were found murdered between two cities, the procedure was to measure from the body to each of those cities, and the city closest was the one whose elders bore the guilt for the murder. We read in Deuteronomy:

"If anyone is found slain, lying in the field in the land which the Lord your God is giving you to possess, and it is not known who killed him,

then your elders and your judges shall go out and measure the distance from the slain man to the surrounding cities.

And it shall be that the elders of the city nearest to the slain man will take a heifer which has not been worked and has not pulled with a yoke.

The elders of that city shall bring the heifer down to a valley with flowing water, which is neither plowed nor sown, and they shall break the heifer's neck there in the valley.

Then the priests, the sons of Levi, shall come near, for the Lord your God has chosen them to minister to Him and to bless the name of the Lord; by their word every controversy and every assault shall be settled.

And all the elders of that city nearest to the slain man shall wash their hands over the heifer whose neck was broken in the valley.

Then they shall answer and say, 'Our hands have not shed this blood, nor have our eyes seen it.

Provide atonement, O Lord, for Your people Israel, whom You have redeemed, and do not lay innocent blood to the charge of Your people Israel.' And atonement shall be provided on their behalf for the blood" (Deuteronomy 21:1-8 NKJV).

The rabbis then commented that if the elders were of the proper level of holiness and sought justice as they should, then God Himself would prevent such a thing from happening on their watch. That the King of glory could be unjustly executed on the watch of such great men as Rabbi Gamaliel only goes to show the point all the more—that though they had much correct, they still were not seeking justice as they should.

If you have spent any time in Israel or among the Jewish people, you know that there is no such thing as keeping something quiet. The rabbis have a statement: "A matter is only a secret so long as only one knows, once it becomes two the whole world knows." It is doubtful that the plot to kill Jesus was not known abroad, especially in the hallowed halls of power. While there were many reasons for someone who did not believe in Jesus not to get involved, not a single one of those reasons could satisfy the demands of justice. Tragically, to fully elucidate roles and responsibilities of elders will take an article all its own.

It does serve to state that for the Pharisees it was also politically expedient to allow Jesus to be executed. In the Talmud[16] the rabbis discuss biblical prophecies concerning the end of days that seem to contradict one another, such as the destruction of Damascus (see Isaiah 17) and the highway of the Lord (see Isaiah 19), as well as the divergent ways in which the Messiah was to come, on a donkey (see Zechariah 9:9) or

---

16   Antiquities of the Jews 20:200

in the clouds (see Daniel 7:13). The rabbis, a generation before Jesus, decided that if Israel was worthy, the Messiah would come with the clouds, and if they were not worthy He would come on a donkey. Now we know from the account in Revelation that both of these are true—that His first coming would be on a donkey and His second coming would be in the clouds.[17] However, when Jesus came riding into Jerusalem on a donkey, He was boldly proclaiming to the rabbis in those days, at least in their own minds, that they were not worthy of Him. To them, this was a mortal insult, and it would be most convenient if the Sadducees did away with the problem for them. If He turned out to be the Messiah, then He would surely (in their minds) do away with the Sadducees, which would be equally convenient.

It will always be a temptation for us to allow such expediency to rule the day. It would be incredibly easy for elders and leaders to use their power to judge disputes and call their people to account in order to serve their perceived needs or theological bent. However, this is a perversion of justice beyond measure. The power and authority given to the elders of the church to judge God's own children is not there for them to settle their personal problems and vendettas as best suits their current needs. Rather, we need to learn from the very mistake that put the Lord of glory on the cross and never repeat the act.

---

17   This also teaches us that simply because the Scripture seems to contradict itself, it does not mean that the truth has to be one way or another; quite the opposite, it can be both at different times to serve God's purposes.

CHAPTER TWO

JESUS WAS NOT PLAN B: A GLIMPSE OF GOD'S LOVE

UNDERSTANDING HOW JUSTICE CAN GO wrong and be perverted is incredibly important. If we can adequately learn from the mistakes of the past, it will enable us to guard against repeating those mistakes again. However, more important is having a system of justice that is built upon the proper foundation. As Christians, that foundation should be the finished work of Christ. Therefore, having a firm understanding of the sacrifice of Christ, and all that it accomplished, is of the utmost importance.

While I was in Israel, I was in a Jewish school reviewing a rabbinic text called "Tree of Life," and two particular lines essentially jumped off the page at me:

> *When a desire arose in the Holy One Blessed is He to create the universe, in order that He could be good to His creation, and that they would realize His greatness and that they would merit to be a vehicle for His presence through adherence to the Blessed One. For how could He be called loving, gracious, and merciful, with nothing to show His love, grace, or mercy.*

This statement struck me for several reasons. Foremost was that it answered all of the classic questions of man in just a couple of lines. Those questions being: "Why are we here?" and "What is our purpose?" The basic universal questions that scholars and philosophers have poured over for centuries are answered by this one sentence: We are here because God created us to be good to us, and our purpose is to be lovingly bonded with Him so that He might dwell through us.

Far more than simple philosophical satisfaction, I was profoundly moved in my spirit and felt that there was a truth contained within those lines which were necessary for a full understanding of my relationship with God. However, this is not to say that I ascribe any kind of biblical type authority to the writings of the rabbis. However, many times I find that God uses them to point out to me biblical truths that I have been missing. In this case, as I meditated upon what God was trying to say to me, I came to the realization that the Lord of glory created mankind in order to die for them. On a more personal level, the Father created you and me so that He could send the Son to die for us!

I had always believed quite the opposite of this. My initial understanding of the redeeming work of Christ went something like this: God had created man pure and sinless; however, soon after this blessed event, God's plan took a major detour. Mankind, not entirely happy with the perfect creation God had given them, disobeyed by eating from the fruit of the Tree of the Knowledge of Good and Evil. This started a downward spiral of mankind that God tried to fix numerous times through flood and covenants until the truth of the matter became clear—mankind was incapable of perfection on his own. To rectify this, God held some kind of council within Himself in an attempt to figure out how to finally fix mankind. At some point within this council, the Son, the Lord Jesus preincarnate, came trembling forward and offered to empty Himself of divinity, live a perfect life, and suffer and die for humanity, so that mankind could finally come into perfect relationship with God.

That is a great story; however, one must ask if it is biblically accurate. I believe that it is not. Rather, I believe the biblical message states that man was never in a position in which he could have a full relationship with God strictly under his own abilities. We must look beyond the first two chapters of Genesis to understand what man's standing was when he was created, as it is the testimony of the entirety of Scripture that we build our understanding upon.

The Scripture states concerning man, "What is a mortal that You should bear him in mind, and a child of mankind that You should consider him? For You have caused him to be made little lower than the angels, yet with glory and honor You have crowned him" (see Psalm 8:4-5).

Here we see that for whatever reason, humanity was created on a level even lower than God's holy angels. At our best, before sin entered mankind, the angels were still somehow on a level higher than mankind. So then let us look at the place which the angels themselves occupied. "Behold in His servants He cannot place trust, and to His angels He ascribes error" (see Job 4:18). Even the Lord's present heavenly servants and angels have no integrity in His sight. Even they are filled with error. Later it says, "Behold, He can put no trust in His holy ones; even the heavens have no merit in His eyes" (see Job 15:15). Quite simply, if man was created lower than the angels, and even they are charged with error by God, then mankind also would have to be impure and filled with error in God's sight. Whether we are in our current fallen state or in the pre-fallen state, mankind simply needed something to lift him higher in order to have a full relationship with God. If even God's holy habitation, the very heavens, are not worthy of Him, how much less is mankind?

I have often heard that the position of mankind as being below the angels is the result of being sinful beings. However, when Jesus emptied Himself of His divinity, He also became lower than the angels.

But stripped Himself [of all privileges and rightful dignity], so as to assume the guise of a servant (slave), in that He became like men and was born a human being (Philippians 2:7 AMP).

For some little time You have ranked him lower than and inferior to the angels; You have crowned him with glory and honor and set him over the works of Your hands,

for You have put everything in subjection under his feet. Now in putting everything in subjection to man, He left nothing outside [of man's] control. But at present we do not yet see all things subjected to him [man].

But we are able to see Jesus, Who was ranked lower than the angels for a little while, crowned with glory and honor because of His having suffered death, in order that by the grace (un-merited favor) of God [to us sinners] He might experience death for every individual person (Hebrews 2:7-9 AMP).

Even Jesus, of whom we can ascribe no sin, had to lower Himself below the angels to become man in order that God's ultimate plan could be carried out. Mankind's initial position of being lower than the angels had nothing to do with sin, but was rather God's initial created order of things. As the Book of Hebrews clearly states: His plan was to lift us up from our position and make all things subject to man. In order to do that, God had to lift man higher than he could ever reach on his own. Leviticus states:

"So the priest who is anointed and ordained to serve as priest in his father's place shall make atonement: he shall thus put on the linen garments, the holy garments,

and make atonement for the holy sanctuary, and he shall make atonement for the tent of meeting and for the altar. He shall also make atonement for the priests and for all the people of the assembly" (Leviticus 16:32-33).

It is understandable that the priest had to make atonement for the people. However, that he also had to make atonement for the very Holy of Holies baffles the mind. The Holy of Holies contained such a level of sanctity that no one but the high priest was to enter it, and even then only on the day of Yom Kippur. Then if he was lacking in due holiness at all, he would be killed—not by men, but by God.

Everything to this point shows that man, even before the Fall, was incapable of having a perfect relationship with God on his own. If even the very heavens and the Holy of Holies are impure and in need of atonement before God, both which sin has never touched, how much more was man in need of atonement before God, before the Fall, and all the more so after?

The Lord of all is an infinitely perfect being incapable of any error. Simply put, no created thing could ever reach that level of perfection without God's help. God, being omniscient, knew that man would never be able to attain the perfection that would be required for perfect relationship. This is not to say that God caused man to sin, or that God set man up for the rebellion that was the eating of the Tree of the Knowledge of Good and Evil, but rather that God knew that man, even at his best, would still be imperfect and flawed.

The Hebrew language, and thus the Old Testament, contains seven different words for sin. They range in intensity from active rebellion, to error, to simple imperfection. The sin of Adam that caused the Fall, the active rebellion against God's direct decree to abstain from eating the fruit of the tree, was an act that further lowered the state of all mankind. However, the point still remains that aside from this act, mankind was still not perfect. The rebellion of man was simply a symptom of a deeper problem inherent in all of creation. The passages from Job which state that the heavens and His holy angels are impure, untrustworthy, and full of error, illustrates this point the best. We are not talking about devils, demons, and unclean spirits, which were cast down, but rather we are speaking of the very angels that minister before the throne.

Long before the Creator began His creation, He knew He had full knowledge that on its own, His creation from greatest to lowest would never be worthy of having full relationship with Him. Yet it was that very relationship that God desired to have with man. Thus the plan was formed:

But [you were purchased] with the precious blood of Christ (the Messiah), like that of a [sacrificial] lamb without blemish or spot.

It is true that He was chosen and foreordained (destined and foreknown for it) before the foundation of the world, but He was brought out to public view (made manifest) in these last days (at the end of the times) for the sake of you (I Peter 1:19-20 AMP).

Before God even spoke the first word of creation, He had already planned to make the ultimate sacrifice for mankind. Eugene Peterson in his paraphrase of this verse puts it exquisitely:

Your life is a journey you must travel with a deep consciousness of God. It cost God plenty to get you out of that dead-end, empty-headed life you grew up in. He paid with Christ's sacred blood, you know. He died like an unblemished, sacrificial lamb. And this was no afterthought. Even though it has only lately—at the end of the ages—become public knowledge, God always knew he was going to do this for you. It's because of this sacrificed Messiah, whom God then raised from the dead and glorified, that you trust God, that you know you have a future in God (I Peter 1:19 The Message).

One of the greatest ways of arrogance within humanity is to think that we can forcibly change God's plans or throw them into disarray. I do not believe that God was in heaven wringing His hands when mankind rebelled against Him in the Garden of Eden, and then scrambling to find a solution to a world thrown in disarray. At worst, mankind only complicated things for themselves. In the story of Jonah, God's plan was for Jonah to travel from Jerusalem (point A) to Nineveh (point B) to preach His Word. All that Jonah's rebellion did was create a large detour which included being swallowed by a fish and vomited back up. In other words, he caused a great deal of mess for himself, but in the end, God's plan was completed.

I cannot say that I know how things would have worked out with the sacrifice of the Son if mankind had not rebelled in the Garden. It is clear that there probably would not have been Romans, Pharisees, Sadducees, and all the other players of the day. It may or may not have taken so many thousands of years from the creation of mankind to perform, but I am sure that it would have happened. I do know that the picture of God's love and goodness painted here is unspeakable. **"No one has greater love [no one has shown stronger affection] than to lay down (give up) his own life for his friends" (John 15:13 AMP).** Not only is this sacrifice by itself amazing—that someone would willingly give up his life for another—but the fact that God created His friends, you and me, for that very purpose is beyond amazing.

As I was sitting in a two-thousand year old school in the middle of the Old City of Jerusalem, it was not just what I was reading that inspired me, but what the Spirit was speaking to me. It went something like this: *A desire arose in the Holy One Blessed to create the universe, in order that He could be good to His creation, by laying down His own life that they may be fully counted as His friends and have perfect relationship with Him. That they would realize His greatness and that they would merit to be a vehicle for His presence through His loving sacrifice for them and thus our loving adherence to the Blessed One.*

CHAPTER THREE
THE NEED FOR JUSTICE

MANY OF US HAVE SEEN A SITUATION IN which one Christian had a complaint with another, but with nowhere to seek a proper solution. Often, one of two things will occur: Either the matter is settled in a secular court, or grace is given when justice is needed. Either way this is a defeat. For a brother or sister in the faith to act with anything less than the utmost integrity toward another is already a loss. Even though the one who forgives may grow in grace, for such things to go uncorrected and be put on display to the world gives the enemy a victory through injustice.

The primary aspects of our lives where we need justice to be present when we fail are our financial dealings and our moral dealings. Genesis 6:13 states: "The end of all flesh has come before me; for the land is filled with robbery because of them" (translation my own). The Hebrew word that is translated as robbery here is *chamas*, which can also mean injustice. It is often translated as violence in many Christian Bibles; however, that is not really accurate though injustice can be considered a form of violence. If we read this literally, God is saying that He destroyed the world because theft was allowed to go unchecked and justice was not in the land.

As the body of Christ, we are called to be part of a system of restoration to the fallen world, not part of its destruction. How then are we to proceed? In the beginning, the church borrowed its system of government from the Jewish people, or rather had it implanted by a Jewish judge named Paul. As I am both a Jew and a rabbi, that seems a good place to start.

In the Book of Exodus, Jethro counsels Moses to appoint judges. He makes a very clear distinction as to who these judges should be: **"able men who fear God, men of truth, those who hate dishonest gain" (see Exodus 18:21).** God tells Moses, **"Gather for Me seventy men from the elders of Israel" (see Numbers 11:16).** Moses brought the number to seventy-one and constituted the first Sanhedrin. By the time of Jesus, the Jewish court system had expanded significantly. There was the Sanhedrin, the court of seventy-one, who ordained all other Jewish judges throughout the world. This court of seventy-one alone could rule on capital offenses. Below them were the lesser Sanhedrins—courts consisting of thirty-five judges. These operated only in Israel and were established over regions. These courts were authorized to mete out corporal punishments, but not capital punishments. Finally, there were the lesser courts. These were tribunals (courts of three judges) set up in each city, and they had the ability to only hand out financial punishment such as fines.

The Jewish courts of today derive their powers from these lesser courts of old, though their powers now are somewhat decreased. According to rabbinic commentary (Gittin 88B), the Sanhedrin and also the lesser courts are authorized by the Torah to hear cases and hand down verdicts only if they have ordination from Sanhedrin level judges. Before someone can become a fully qualified judge and thus be able to hand out punitive fines or corporal or capital punishment, he must be ordained by someone who is qualified to sit upon the Sanhedrin. Therefore, in the earlier stages of Israel's history this authority was handed down from one generation to the next. However, in 450 A.D., the Sanhedrin was officially disbanded and this ordination ceased. Thus in many ways the judges of Israel and the Jewish people today are but a shadow of the judges of old. Since there is still a need for justice, there is still a need for these religious judges. As we still retain some of our old authority, we still have the ability to hear certain cases. The judges today have powers only in the following instances and with the following restrictions:

Monetary cases

(1) Must arise often (monetary claims, etc.)

(2) Must involve monetary loss to the claimant

(3) Cannot impose punitive fines

Moral failure

(1) Can impose communal and/or ministerial restrictions

(2) Can impose excommunication

(3) Can invoke *Tzliphot D'Aish* (defined below)

Marital issues

(1) Conflict resolution

(2) Divorce

For example, if person X claims that person Y owes him money and witnesses are ready to testify that in their presence, Y admitted he borrowed and did not repay or alternatively they were present when Y took the loan, then the court can rule and impose a fine which would cover the monetary loss. The fine, however, cannot be for more than the amount still owed.

If a person is found in a moral failure or ongoing sin, and there are two or more witnesses to establish this, then the court will first impose communal, and if applicable, ministerial restrictions upon the person in an attempt to bring them to restoration. If the person does not repent, rejects those restrictions, and continues on in their error, the court can impose a *cherem,* or excision, from the community. This means that it is made public that the person is in sin (though the sin, the nature of the sin, and its details are not revealed) and that the community is no longer to have any relations or dealings of any kind with this person until they return to the court, repent, and accept its decisions.

If all of this fails to bring the person to repentance, there is one option left to the court, and it is only with much trepidation, hesitation, fear, and trembling that I make mention of it. When all of these attempts have been given sufficient time to work their cure and still have had no effect, having given the person sufficient warning as to their last resort, the court could invoke the *Tzliphot D'Aish,* which is Hebrew for "wisps of fire." This is an ancient rabbinical prayer which is never entered into lightly. The introduction and instruction that precedes the prayer reads, "Know before whom it is that you stand, King who reigns over kings, the Holy One Blessed be He. Know that when one invokes this prayer the Lord stands in judgment and weighs in His perfect scales the invoker against the accused. Whoever is found wicked, even by a hair's breath, upon him the judgment will fall. If they are found to be equal, the judgment reverts back to the invoker, as is the case with those who falsely accuse."

The use of this is almost never done. Paul is recorded as having used this prayer or something similar when he states that he handed a certain individual over to Satan (see I Corinthians 5:5). Judaism believes that the very second a person begins to repent, they are deemed by heaven as completely righteous, so it is easy to see why this step is enacted so infrequently. Essentially, the hope is that by experiencing a little of hell (hence wisps of fire) in this life, the person will repent.

The prayer itself is simply composed of a number of Psalms interspersed with prayers that the wicked person would only suffer to the point of repentance. However, as it is considered to be a somewhat dangerous prayer, and the fact that the rabbis do not want it to be abused as a curse, thrown around in a twisted attempt at revenge, the exact formula of this liturgical prayer has never been made public knowledge. It is typically only handed down to qualified judges and rabbis who are deemed to be of sufficient spiritual maturity to deal with the responsibility of it properly. For that reason, I have also chosen not to include it here.

There is one last situation that our religious courts deal with, which is probably the most important of them all—broken marriages. Judaism, in allowing for divorce, is in my opinion uniquely suited to deal with it. From the start, it should be stated that while Judaism allows for divorce for a myriad of reasons, it considers all divorce, no matter the reason, a grievous sin. Unlike any other case that may rise before the court, here the judges begin to spiritually prepare themselves days in advance. They fast on nothing but water for the three days prior to the case and are on a complete fast (no water either) on the day of the case. In addition, during their regular prayer times, they say a number of added prayers called *slichot*, which are special and detailed prayers of repentance. The rabbi who officiated the wedding is called to appear before the court as well, as he is considered to be responsible for the condition of the marriage and in seeing to its health. Except in extreme cases, even if infidelity was involved, the court never grants a divorce at the first hearing. Rather, they attempt every avenue of restoration possible first.

The rabbi who officiated the wedding is expected, if at all possible, to oversee the restoration process. If for some reason it is truly impossible for him to do so, then the court will appoint another trusted rabbi. Only after every avenue and possibility for reconciliation has been fully tried and exhausted will the divorce be granted. In this regrettable case, a divorce ceremony known as a *Get* takes place. However, anyone whom I have ever spoken with who has gone through a *Get* has always said the same thing—that they would suffer any torture or discomfort which can be meted out on this earth before they would ever do it again. The ceremony is designed to be a quick and complete severing of the relationship with the full knowledge of both parties. As such, it is also very shocking and emotionally painful.

A *Get* ceremony is rather involved. As already stated, it is a day of fasting and repentance. The couple to be divorced comes to the court, which is held in the sanctuary of a synagogue. There they sit before a tribunal of judges, who ask questions as to why the marriage has failed. They listen to the testimony of the couple and the rabbis involved. Once they are certain that the only course left for the marriage is to dissolve the relationship,[18] they move into the formal ceremony. At this point, the judges inform the couple as to exactly what divorce means, scripturally and by Jewish law. They inform the couple that the dissolution of their marriage will very likely preclude them from remarrying if they should later have a change of heart. They also lay down a time period in which they are not to engage in other romantic relationships. They are then told that they are going to be asked a series of questions and instructed to answer only with a simple yes or no. Anything beyond this is considered a vow, and as they are already breaking one commitment, this is not the time to be binding oneself with a vow.

From this point forward, the divorce becomes very ceremonial and symbolic. Each is asked if they are making this decision under any kind of duress. They are asked if they truly intend to divorce. They are asked if they have understood all of the instructions so far. Finally, they are told that from this point forward they are forbidden to ever say they were not divorced, or that they had no intention of divorce, or that they did not want the divorce in some way. Then they are asked if they understand

---

18   This is sixty days for men and ninety for women. The additional thirty days for women is not a gender bias, but to ensure that she is not pregnant from the current marriage, so as the status of the child will not be in question.

this. Assuming that all answers are in the affirmative, the divorce proceeds.

A scribe is now brought in to write the actual *Get*. As a *Get* is a legal document, certain procedures, clauses, and so forth have to be adhered to. In many ways in Judaism, marriage, though a covenant, is truly a contractual agreement in which the stipulations of the marriage, duties of husband and wife, and also inheritance issues are laid out. It has always struck me as odd that a wedding contract, or *Ketubah,* can be printed on something as small as a typical sheet of typing paper, while a *Get*, the document that effectually severs all that is written in rather fine print, is on a sheet of paper at least a meter square. It has also always struck me odd that if a mistake[19] is made in the *Ketubah*, there is no problem; it is still valid as is the marriage. However, a single mistake in the *Get* invalidates the entire divorce. The couple is told to instruct the scribe that he has their permission to write up to one-thousand copies to achieve one that is totally correct.

Once the *Get* has been written, a process which takes some time, the final stage of the divorce commences. In Judaism, because of the prenuptial agreement and other things, there are no messy court cases and fights over division of property. The court, i.e., the tribunal of judges, arbitrarily decides and follows the terms of the prenuptial.

---

19   Things such as spelling errors, and such.

Then, based on a number of factors, they decide how to divide anything not covered by the prenuptial, such as child custody and so forth. As entire books have been written on this subject, which deal with the hows, whys, and what ifs, there simply is not space here to elaborate. Suffice it to say that as advocating a case is forbidden in the Jewish world, decisions are made on sound biblical reasoning.[20] The document now written is folded a specific way and handed to the husband. He is then instructed to face his wife and to drop it into her outstretched hands. Once done, he says the words, "I release you; you are released from me and free to marry another." The wife then turns and walks a certain distance away, approximately two meters, and turns back to the husband and says, "I release you; you are released and free to marry another." This final step, from what I understand, though it sounds simple in print, has saved many marriages. At this point, the divorce is over and the former couple is free to continue about their way.

---

20   In Jewish law it is forbidden to view any two cases the same. Thus, precedent law as in the United States is non-existent. There are traditions on how different situations are to be handled, but those are pure cases. They also do not deal with the many "what ifs" that come up in everyday life. Thus, it is the responsibility of the judges to look at each case from every possible angle, and prayerfully and fearfully enter into judgment. In the case of divorce, they look first to protect any children that may be affected, and then a fair division of assets. That last statement is trickier. A man is required, if he divorces his wife for any reason other than marital unfaithfulness, to pay her Ketubah price, typically, approximately $200,000. Any further division of assets will only occur if the husband's remaining assets are greater. Beyond that the details get very complicated.

CHAPTER FOUR

THE INNER WORKINGS OF JEWISH JUSTICE

U P UNTIL NOW, THE DISCUSSION HAS focused mainly on what the courts do and how they hear cases. At this point, the discussion will progress with the way in which the courts operate. These courts are constituted by a number of different people: an Av Beit Din or "father of the court," judges, a scribe, witnesses, and litigants. Let us look at who each of these people are at slightly greater length.

The Av Bet Din is the chief judge of the court. He receives his status by being elected to it by the other judges. Typically, the Av is considered by his peers as being the most righteous and wise among them. This is not to state that judges are all men; I only use this term for ease of writing. In fact, some judges and heads of courts in Israel are women—in this case called an *Em*, "mother." The Av is afforded no more authority than any other judge. Rather, his position is more typically like that of an administrator. It is his job to schedule hearings and judges, to oversee payment of court costs, and other such dealings.

The real backbone of the court, what truly establishes and ensures its holiness and success, are its judges. These judges are not ordinary men, but rather the learned and wise elders of Israel. First, to begin training as a judge, you have to become an ordained rabbi in one of the four main areas of Torah that still apply to every Jew today. This takes about three to five years of intense study which then culminates in days of grueling exams where you are expected to have firmly memorized everything that you have learned from day one. The lecture you received and the texts which you read on the first day must be as familiar and known as well as those you memorized on the last day. It is important to note that Judaism does not consider a subject truly learned unless the text has been completely memorized. Only once you have passed these tests are you qualified to begin training as a judge.

Judicial training in Judaism is much like rabbinic training, only there is a requirement to learn three times the information, mostly on justice with monetary laws, marriage, and divorce laws thrown in. The process of learning this information takes at least eight years. At the end, and assuming the tests are passed, you will be taken into the sanctuary that serves also as the court. You will be given a Torah scroll to hold and among many other words, you will be charged with the following : "This is the Torah of the Lord, which He gave through

His servant Moses; it is a tree of life to those that take hold of it. You have been entrusted as a guardian of the Holy flame; keep it until the days of the Messiah and the world to come, at which point God will demand an accounting for every decision you have made[21]." At which point the judge to be can either decline and walk away or declare, "Yes, may it be His will; all this I will accept and more if God so decrees. Amen and Amen." Then hands will be laid upon him, and he will have joined the ranks of the judges. He may now sit as a part of a tribunal and hear cases.

A Higher Standard

One final point about judges—they are expected to live at the highest standards of integrity and morality. It was stated earlier that the courts typically do not reveal any of the details of a person's sin or moral failing. The only exception is in the case of a judge. Because of the authority and responsibility to which they have aspired, they are expected to live at a level of integrity and morality in

---

21   An interesting vestige of this has been preserved in the Eastern Orthodox Church. There when a priest or bishop is ordained, in the midst of the ceremony, communion is served. In the Eastern Church, they use an actual loaf of bread. The officiant takes a piece of the bread and places it into the hand of one being ordained. Then he states, "This is the body of Christ, His people and the sheep of His pasture, take it and guard it until the second coming of Christ at which time He will demand it back from you with an accounting." I cannot help but wonder if we in the West have lost something by dropping this from our own ordination services.

keeping with their position. If they are found in a failing of integrity, morality, or abuse of power, the sin and all of its details are made public and broadcast widely.

Announcements would be made and notices posted in every synagogue within the judge's jurisdiction precisely detailing the error. The heads of other jurisdictions would be immediately notified as well and given the same announcements posted within a jurisdiction. If the now former judge was found to be moving to an area, every rabbi in the area would be notified as to his behavior. This may sound harsh, and to a certain extent it is. However, it is done to instill an awesome fear of sin within the community, especially the judges themselves, as well as to convey the awesome authority and responsibility imparted while giving ample incentive to never fail it. As a side note and a testimony to its deterrent ability, this action has in fact only been taken three times in the last seven hundred years of Jewish history.

The Scribes

The scribe has a very straightforward job—to write the decision of the court. Often the scribe does this while the judges are preparing the litigants and witnesses for the next case before them. Scribes typically drafted bills of divorce that could then be witnessed and attested to by the judges. In Jewish court, this is still always done with a quill and parchment. Great care is taken to ensure that every detail of the documents is exact and precise.

The Witnesses

The witnesses are second only to the judges in importance. It is solely upon their testimony that a case is decided. For this reason they also must be people of integrity. Witnesses are never permitted to be related, indebted, or in any other financial or familial way aligned to either of the litigants so that they will not be tempted to pervert their testimony and thus pervert justice. There always needs to be at least two witnesses to establish testimony as correct. Jewish law does not allow any physical, video, or other evidence to be entered into the court unless there are witnesses to confirm it.

Just as judges have additional responsibilities and thus are held to a certain standard, so are witnesses. Witnesses must be of the faith and without ongoing sin or moral failure in their lives; any of these things will disqualify them and nullify their testimony. New converts and heathen are not trusted in their testimony and thus are not valid witnesses. In most cases, children under a certain age also are not accepted as valid witnesses. Finally, if a witness is found to have intentionally falsified his testimony, the form of punishment that would have fallen on the litigant is imposed upon him.

Within the Jewish court we have litigants. Most unique in Jewish courts is the fact that litigants are not allowed to testify. Though they may be questioned by the judges, they are not permitted to attempt to build a case for themselves. Their testimony is not considered valid above that of the witnesses; rather, it can only give additional information. Even an admission of guilt or debt is only valid if witnesses can attest to it. The primary purpose of the litigants is to lodge complaints and professions of guilt or innocence.

Present Limitations

The system has some present limitations because we no longer live in the perfect theocracy. We no longer have God-appointed kings, priests, and judges as the rulers of our nation. Today we live under a secular government which typically has very little respect for those who seek to follow the Lord. Without a way to enforce its decisions, a Jewish court would simply be a paper tiger. It would look good but generally be ineffective. This does not alleviate the command given to the Jews to only enter into law in a religious court. A rabbinic commentary found in the Talmud Niddah 66B states, "Even if we are certain that a secular court would rule exactly the same as our own courts, we are still forbidden to go to them for they do not fear God and it would be a blasphemy." To a Jew, this is not a polite suggestion on how to ideally do things; instead it is an absolute imperative. Therefore, there must be found a way to give teeth to the tiger.

As I am an Israeli-ordained United States rabbi, I can only speak of how things are done in those specific countries to effectuate this process. For spatial reasons, I will only touch here on the system in the United States. In the United States, there is a legal loophole which allows for citizens to settle their differences out of court, yet retain the same enforceability as if it had been decided within a court of the United States. This is called a binding arbitration. Two citizens can at the outset of a marriage, business transaction, or any other matter that would be settled in a civil court, agree to have the matter settled by a pre-determined arbitrator should something go wrong. That arbitrator or its appointees have the legally binding ability to settle the issues at hand.

With the unprecedented religious freedom and the freedom that exists in the United States, typically the decisions of a religious institution have no real hold on the individual. Rather, they can simply pick up and go to a different area or assembly and leave it all behind. That is not the case here. Instead, if the person should be so lacking in integrity as to try to escape justice, even that which is handed down from their religious authorities, a binding arbitration agreement makes the decision legally enforceable. To put that into layman's terms, the secular justice system can be brought in, and they will have no choice but to uphold the decision of the religious court. In this way there is truly nowhere a citizen of the United States can go that he or she will be free from this decision.

To put all of this into a practical application, in the Jewish world no business is transacted with another Jew unless a binding arbitration agreement is signed first. This is a fairly simple process of having the agreement signed, witnessed, and notarized, and then delivered into the hands of the court prior to the signing of the contract. No marriage will be performed without a binding arbitration agreement being signed beforehand in place of a prenuptial agreement, giving all authority over the dissolution of the marriage, the division of assets, and custody of children into the hands of the religious courts.

In this way, the sanctity of justice is maintained within the religious community. The regrettable event is kept from the eyes of the world, but not swept under the rug. Rather, it is dealt with in a way befitting the people of God. This also serves a second purpose which is vitally important in the life and vibrancy of Judaism—it makes the religious life and community not just an accessory to their lifestyle, but the very center and focus of it. The only thing that the religious court cannot arbitrate is criminal offenses.

There is one last thing that needs to be touched upon before I delve into the New Testament on this subject. Jewish courts are by no means punitive in nature. Jewish law forbids it within the current situation, as discussed earlier. More than that, we see ourselves as being vitally involved with a ministry of justice through righteousness, reconciliation, and restoration. This is derived through an interesting logical progression.

The rabbis look first at the Scriptures which seem to indicate that originally the priests were the judges in Israel (see Deuteronomy 17:9). According to rabbinical tradition, only after the priest had properly instructed the elders could they become judges. They then ask: Who are these priests, and from where did they derive their authority? That is easy enough to answer: They were sons of Aaron. Finally, they ask: Why was Aaron chosen out of all of Israel and out of all of the Levites to be the father of all the priests? The rabbis answer that in a commentary called Pirke Avot, "Ethics of our Fathers" 1:14, "Aaron loved peace and he pursued it, and he loved people and he brought them close to the Scripture and to God." Since as a father he passed down these same qualities in others, those others would also make excellent judges. Thus to the Jewish people, the real purpose of our judges is to make peace between them and to bring individuals close to Scripture and to God.

While Christians are by no means bound by Jewish law and therefore could, if they wished, establish punitive courts, I would personally urge against it. Punitive courts, in my opinion, would only hinder the ministry of reconciliation and restoration that the church is called to. While there are measures that must be taken when a member of the community falls into sin in order to bring correction, repentance, and ultimately restoration, when it is brother contending with brother over the temporal things of this world, the ministry of reconciliation and restoration is much more easily accomplished if punitive damages are not a possibility.

I believe that the system outlined above can also be found in the New Testament and will work well with New Testament principles. The idea in the following paragraphs is to delve through the New Testament and show how a rabbi would read it and possibly what was going through the minds of the writers, most especially Paul. Hopefully, this will help to lay a cornerstone for the beginning of a viable model for the church to begin to build a system of courts and justice within it.

The first passage is Matthew 18:15, **"If your brother sins against you, go and show him his fault, just between the two of you. If he listens to you, you have won your brother over"** (NIV). Jesus is stating here that even though we have courts (remember He is speaking to a Jewish audience for whom these courts would have been a way of life), we are not to immediately run off to them as soon as there is a problem. Rather, we should first start by going to the brother and trying to reason with him, and hopefully it will have to go no further. **"But if he will not listen, take one or two others along, so that every matter may be established by the testimony of two or three witnesses"** (Matthew 18:16 NIV). Here, we are starting the formal process of court hearings. We are bringing valid witnesses into the situation.

Still, you will notice that the hope is to avoid having to take the matter into the court, but if that becomes a necessity, then the preparations have been made. It is also important to note that witnesses are supposed to warn the party at fault about what their actions are leading them to and if possible (in the case of some sins) to restrain them. Without this in Judaism, they are not considered valid witnesses. **"If he refuses to listen to them, tell it to the church: and if he refuses to listen even to the church, treat him as you would a pagan or a tax collector" (Matthew 18:17 NIV).** If the warning of the witnesses does not work, then we can take it to the church. Here I believe that Jesus is not saying to go pronounce it to the entire congregation, but bearing in mind that the communal court was within the walls of the "church," He was telling them to go to the court. Even then, if the court's decision was rejected (they did not have binding arbitration), then they should treat them with the process with which we would deal with a sinner.

"I tell you the truth, whatever you bind on earth will be bound in heaven, and whatever you loose on earth will be loosed in heaven" (Matthew 18:18 NIV). This is probably one of the most powerful Scriptures about Christian authority that I know of. Let me explain this the way I believe a Jew would understand it. Binding and loosing in Jewish legal thought typically means permitting or forbidding. In fact, the section of law that one has to learn to become a rabbi is called *issur v'heter*, and in English "bound and loosed." In Jewish thought, rabbinic authority imbues one with the ability to forbid or permit things as new situations arise, especially those that were not problems in biblical times.[22] Let us now turn to Paul's first letter to the Corinthians.

> **Does any one of you, when he has a case against his neighbor, dare to go to law before the unrighteous, and not before the saints?**
>
> **Or do you not know that the saints will judge the world? And if the world is judged by you, are you not competent to constitute the smallest law courts?**
>
> **Do you not know that we shall judge angels? How much more, matters of this life?**
>
> **If then you have law courts dealing with matters of this life, do you appoint them as judges who are of no account in the church?**
>
> **I say this to your shame. Is it so, that there is not among you one wise man who will be able to decide between his brethren,**
>
> **but brother goes to law with brother, and that before unbelievers? (I Corinthians 6:1-6)**

---

22 The Internet is a good modern example, considering that the Internet in many ways is like both heaven and hell. Things can be found that are incredibly uplifting and also incredibly perverse. Rabbis have thus struggled to lay down guidelines for their followers that would help them to live upright lives.

The first thing that springs to mind here is the earlier mentioned commentary found in Gittin 66B: "Even if we are certain that a secular court would rule exactly the same as our own courts, we are still forbidden to go to them for they do not fear God and it would be a blasphemy." Paul is obviously against the idea of believers using a secular court of any sort to settle their differences; rather, he fully expects them to have constituted law courts themselves.

Also, he points out that those appointed as judges need be of some account or importance in the church. We discussed earlier that every city should have a law court and that the elders should sit as judges. I think it is very telling in light of what Paul writes to Titus, **"For this reason I left you in Crete, that you might set in order what remains, and appoint elders in every city as I directed you" (Titus 1:5).** It seems that this was standard operating procedure for Paul.

Paul continues in Corinthians: **"Actually, then, it is already a defeat for you, that you have lawsuits with one another. Why not rather be wronged? Why not rather be defrauded? On the contrary, you yourselves wrong and defraud. You do this even to your brethren" (I Corinthians 6:7-8).** This is an important fact. Our establishing law courts are a way of countering the enemy's attack upon the brotherhood. Paul states that it is a Christian's place to accept the evil of this world, to be defrauded or wronged by the world, and to forgive. However, when a brother uses that against a brother to the hurt of the body, the enemy has won a victory, and this cannot be. Justice is absolutely commanded here to keep the enemy from having victory over the church and for blocking that victory from becoming complete by a brother needing to take a brother before the heathen.

Paul closes out this line of thought with this, to which I need add nothing at this time for it speaks for itself: **"Or do you not know that the unrighteous will not inherit the kingdom of God? Do not be deceived; neither fornicators, nor idolaters, nor adulterers, nor effeminate, nor homosexuals, nor thieves, nor the covetous, nor drunkards, nor revilers, nor swindlers, will inherit the kingdom of God. Such were some of you; but you were washed, but you were sanctified, but you were justified in the name of the Lord Jesus Christ and in the Spirit of our God"** (I Corinthians 6:9-11).

One last Scripture that I want to quote, because it speaks so eloquently of the Jewish position, is I Timothy 5:19-20, **"Do not receive an accusation against an elder except on the basis of two or three witnesses. Those who continue in sin, rebuke in the presence of all, so that the rest also will be fearful of sinning."** We should never entertain any accusation against any member of the body of Christ lightly, but the more so against those who are elders in the body. However, when we become assured that an elder has fallen into sin, it seems that Paul as well declares that the sin of the elder is to be made public.

CHAPTER FIVE

ELDERSHIP

IN ORDER FOR ANY SYSTEM OF JUSTICE TO work, there will need to be those to administrate it. Biblically, those who administrate the justice system are the elders. However, few may understand who an elder is. Often when good teaching comes forth on eldership, many of us shake our heads and say that it is impossible, that the standards are too high. However, with God all things are possible. It is not our place to try to lower His standards, but to have faith in Him to empower us to meet them.

In the 1940s, it was stated that running a mile in less than four minutes was simply impossible. Then in 1954, Roger Bannister ran the first sub-four-minute mile. Within weeks of his accomplishment, his record was broken a number of times and now the sub-four-minute mile is the standard by which competitive middle distance runners are judged. In the same way, the church now needs its Roger Bannister to show that biblical eldership is possible in more than theory. First, let us look at a biblical elder.

Three Levels of Eldership

Let us start by defining what an elder is. Biblically, I believe there can be found three distinct levels of spiritual leadership. These levels are specifically pastors, overseers, and elders. I personally believe that this was based on the Jewish system which also recognizes three distinct levels of spiritual leadership: Mashgiach Ruchani (shortened to MaR), Rabbi, and Dayan. With each of these levels comes distinct powers and responsibilities—each level has its own distinct areas of authority.

The pastor/MaR is primarily responsible for the areas of teaching and leading people into a godly lifestyle and caring for individuals. The primary works of the pastor/MaR are teaching, feeding the sheep, and counseling. They can also ordain worthy individuals to their own level and have the authority to marry with the permission of a rabbi/overseer.

In many ways, the MaR is the real backbone of the community. In every Yeshivah or community that I have been in, it was a rare occasion that a day passed when I did not have some kind of conversation with the MaR. Most often it was to make sure that my marriage was fine, or to get me to have people over for dinner, and various mundane events of the day-to-day life of the community. However, there was one time while I was in Jerusalem that I had skipped evening prayers at the Yeshivah for about a week, and so the MaR came up to me one morning and said that he had noticed that I had not been at the evening prayer services. He wanted to know if I was just praying somewhere else, such as the Western Wall, or if for some reason I was skipping altogether. If that was the case, I should know that skipping prayer is seriously detrimental to one's relationship with God, and without the proper connection to God one simply cannot hope to understand His Word. So it is vital for my success in the Yeshivah (where eight hours a day are devoted to studying the Word) that I not skip prayer. Actually, to this day I cherish that conversation, because while very pointed, it was never expressed in a way that would stir up guilt or condemnation, but rather I felt nothing but concern.

The rabbi/overseer has all of the same responsibilities and authority as the pastor/MaR. In addition, with each level, the amount of work required does not decrease, it increases. In truth, spiritual leaders are all volunteers; there are no drafts; there are no conscripts; each one chooses the level at which they are going to serve. In addition to the previously listed authority and responsibilities, at this level the rabbi/overseer may marry a couple at will. There is a very distinct reason within Judaism why we limit those who may perform marriages. In marrying a couple, we establish a decree that has the weight of Scripture. Essentially, the one performing a marriage is writing Scripture; it is not to be confused with the written Word, but the living epistle that all believers are meant to be. For instance, up to the second before a man and woman are married, a member of the opposite sex can look upon them with desire in their hearts, within reason, and it is completely permissible. If it were not, no one would ever get married. However, the moment the one performing the marriage declares them married, it then becomes a sin for anyone to look upon them with desire in their hearts. This level of authority is not something that we bestow lightly.

An overseer/rabbi also has the ability to make rulings in their specific area of authority, which is also the area that they have been specifically ordained to. For instance, in Judaism there are four specific areas of Jewish law that still apply to every Jew today. So if a rabbi has been ordained in one area, he can make decisions and rulings in his own area, but has no authority in another area of law. To put it into Christian terms: An overseer appointed over the children's ministry has all the authority to dictate policy within the children's ministry, but has no authority to decide issues in the worship ministry. This does not mean that an overseer cannot be ordained to multiple areas of authority. They also have the ability to ordain to their own level.

I have said that each group has the ability to ordain to their own level. It should be noted that in the Jewish system, ordination does not come easily, and it is not given lightly. The English definition of ordination is "to invest officially (as by the laying on of hands) with ministerial or priestly authority; to establish or order by appointment, decree, or law."[23] However, the Hebrew word is *Semicha*, which means to rely upon or lean on. In Jewish thought, the person being ordained is reliant upon the one ordaining him for all authority. Likewise, the one who ordained the person must be able to trust him, as his reputation is now linked with the person they have ordained. There is an intense discipleship process that happens before one person would ordain another.

Third and highest in this order of biblical leadership is the elder/Dayan. From here on I will simply refer to this office as that of elder. Again, elders have all of the responsibilities and authority of the levels below them. They also have several additional abilities. The first is the ability to make legal rulings. As has been discussed in other places in this book, within the system of justice it is the elders who serve as judges. Thus, upon their shoulders falls the authority to make legal rulings within their communities, but also the responsibility to guard against injustice and any perversion of justice. In this role, the elders have the ability to decree a divorce if, heaven forbid, it should become necessary. It is also the responsibility of the elders to set the standard for holy living within their communities. They should be

---

23 *Merriam-Webster*

examples of spiritual maturity. This will be expounded upon as we move on.

The Backbone of the Body

The elders truly are meant to be the backbone of the system of spiritual leadership. We are going to stop here for a time so we can accurately describe what an elder is and give practical examples of elders at work. I will be drawing a good deal from Old Testament sources. It is important to note the system that God set up in the Old Covenant was a shadow and type for the ideal of the kingdom and as such should not be quickly disregarded. While Christians are free from the Law, with all of its ordinances and statutes, this does not give us free reign to throw away God's system of government, especially when we see this same system of government replicated in the New Testament.

The first biblical instruction that we can find concerning an elder comes from God's specific instructions given to Moses on selecting the first judges who would be over His people Israel: **"Furthermore, you shall select out of all the people able men who fear God, men of truth, those who hate dishonest gain; and you shall place these over them, as leaders of thousands, of hundreds, of fifties and of tens"** (Exodus 18:21).

Some explanations are in order here. At first, the statement **"able men"** does not seem to make a great deal of sense. In truth, the Hebrew word translated here for "able" is *chayil,* which is better translated valiant. For example, Scripture calls Benaiah Ben Jehoida a valiant man (see II Samuel 23:20-23). As well as being one of David's generals, he is most especially famous for jumping into a snowy pit with what was probably a rather irate, trapped lion and promptly killing it. Essentially, God told Moses to find people who would look at angry lions like kittens who needed to be put in their place. In truth, this is an incredibly essential quality for an elder. When the sheep start growling, an angry lion in a pit might look like a good tradeoff.

Zadok, the High Priest, was also called a man of valor (see I Chronicles 12:28). He is best known for his actions during the rebellion of David's son Absalom. Instead of cowering or going over to the new regime, which seemed as though it would be the one to stay, he decided to follow David. Not only did he follow David, but he stole the ark from the tabernacle and led the priests after the true king as well. Then he was willing to go back and serve as a spy within Absalom's kingdom for his king (see II Samuel 15). Elders need to be those who have the courage to follow the King when it seems that following the King may not be the wisest thing to do. Elders need to have the internal fortitude and backbone to stand for truth even if all others go astray.

The second requirement is that they **"fear God."** The Hebrew word used here for **"fear"** is *yireh,* and it truly means fear, not abject terror, but the type of primal fear that brings about a very healthy respect. The Lord made this very clear to me one day when I was visiting the zoo. It was feeding time for the lions, and the lion house was packed with people who wanted to see the lions up close at their feeding. After all of the lionesses were brought in and placed within their feeding cages, the male lion made his entrance. This lion came bursting through a door that looked far too small for such a big cat, and then came to a skidding stop just inches from the bars. Everyone in the lion house took a step back. Then the lion let out an earsplitting roar. At that point, I was thanking God with all of my heart for the bars between that lion and me! Quite simply I was made aware that as majestic and beautiful as that lion was, and as safe as I was at the moment, a fear of that great cat rose up in me simply for the power inherent within it. God then spoke to me that this is what it means to fear Him. A respect and terror for the power inherent within God should prevent me from ever putting myself on the wrong side of that power.

Elders are supposed to hate dishonest gain. For those who are entrusted with finances and stand in judgment of financial matters, they must without doubt stand against dishonest gain in every way—not only the dishonest gain of others, which is easy to hate, but the dishonest gain of their own. These have to be people who are scrupulous to see to it that every penny they have has been rightly and honestly earned. I remember when I was just starting my studies as a rabbi, and I was spending some time in New York with one of my teachers who was a *Dayan*, an elder. He bought us both a Snapple iced tea, and it was not until we were several blocks away that he began to count his change and realized that the teller had given him a dime too much. I offhand made a joke that he was now a dime richer. He looked at me with absolute horror and said, "I am not such a wicked man that I would keep another man's wealth," and immediately turned around and went back to the store. He actually had to argue with the cashier to get him to take the dime back; after all it was just a dime, but this man could not countenance even ten cents of dishonest gain.

The next instance that we find in the Scripture is found in Deuteronomy 1:13: **"Choose wise and discerning and experienced men from your tribes, and I will appoint them as your heads."** Here we get a bit more understanding of what the Lord wants us to look for in those who will be appointed as elders. Wisdom and discernment appear to be necessary gifts and talents. As these people are to be the primary shepherds of God's flock and take charge and responsibility over His children, both are indispensable. However, notice also that here we have listed those who have experience. We should not select elders to serve over our congregations who have no experience or proven track record in ministry—especially since elders are to be over the other ministers, they should know how ministry works.

Elders From a New Testament Perspective

Elders were not strictly the purview of the Old Testament. Rather, the practice of ordaining elders and placing them in power over God's people continued well into the New Testament. Paul commands Timothy:

> An overseer, then, must be above reproach, the husband of one wife, temperate, prudent, respectable, hospitable, able to teach,
>
> not addicted to wine or pugnacious, but gentle, uncontentious, free from the love of money.
>
> He must be one who manages his own household well, keeping his children under control with all dignity
>
> (but if a man does not know how to manage his own household, how will he take care of the church of God?),
>
> and not a new convert, lest he become conceited and fall into the condemnation incurred by the devil.
>
> And he must have a good reputation with those outside the church, so that he may not fall into reproach and the snare of the devil.
>
> Deacons likewise must be men of dignity, not double-tongued, or addicted to much wine or fond of sordid gain,

but holding to the mystery of the faith with a clear conscience.

And let these also first be tested; then let them serve as deacons if they are beyond reproach   (I Timothy 3:2-10).

This is quite a list. One can see how it is derived from the earlier lists given in the Old Testament, but at the same time I believe we can see some of the development of this idea from the Old Covenant into the New Covenant. Let us take this list piece by piece and examine what Paul is looking for in those he believes God wants for elders.

"Above reproach:" An elder has to be completely **"above reproach."** This essentially means that when the sniffing dogs start to sniff, there should be no dirt or skeletons hanging around in the closet waiting to be found. We are not talking about the person's pre-Christian life, but their post-Christian life. What went on before one professed Christ has no bearing on the person as a reborn child of God. However, as those who begin to seek leadership in God's kingdom and to exercise authority over God's children, they need to have a straight and holy life. Leaders are expected to have a life which the children of the King are able to emulate. Those who are going to sit and judge the morality of others need to first turn their eyes upon their own lives and judge themselves.

"Husband of one wife:" There has been much discussion about this requirement, and I do not presume to have the final say or that my opinion is absolutely the correct one. Many interpret this to mean that the person cannot have been divorced and remarried. I see several problems with this interpretation. First and foremost, to me, it seems to contradict the overall message of restoration and healing found throughout the Scriptures. Second, by that same reasoning, a widow or widower would also be forbidden to remarry, as they, too, would then have had more than one spouse if they remarry. This then would also be a position contrary to Scripture. Above all, this same standard would in fact disqualify God Himself from ministry as God is divorced: **"And I saw that for all the adulteries of faithless Israel, I had sent her away and given her a writ of divorce, yet her treacherous sister Judah did not fear; but she went and was a harlot also"** (Jeremiah 3:8). Can we truly hold our human leaders to a standard that God could not pass?

From a Jewish perspective, the requirement to be a **"husband of one wife"** was a statement against polygamy. From Jewish history, this requirement came into being by the time of Jesus. The logic behind it was that the created ideal found in Scripture was that of a family consisting of one husband and one wife, i.e. Adam and Eve. However, the rabbis felt that on account of the hardness of men's hearts and their exposure to pagan kingdoms, God allowed them to take more than one wife with certain provisions in place to prevent absolute perversion. Even into the New Testament period, polygamy was an accepted practice among God's people and in the newborn church. A ban on polygamy was first introduced by Rav Amram in 250 A.D. He placed a thousand-year ban on the practice which has been renewed by subsequent generations. The elders of the church put the first ban in effect against polygamy in the 300s. Today, we do not see polygamy as a daily way of life, but when the Scriptures were written, it was. However, early on the leaders realized God's ideal was not found in the allowances, but in the way in which He originally created mankind. Thus, early on the requirement was placed upon those who would be leaders to live up to that ideal and to show the people the proper path to holiness. It is in this light that I believe this statement by Paul should be interpreted.

"Temperate:" A leader, who is going to hold such authority, must be a person who is temperate. Temperate simply means that a person is not given to extremes or rapidly changing emotions. This is not to say that a temperate person is not passionate to experience strong emotions in their place, but rather that they are not given over to their emotions. The mind controls the expression of the heart. In the realm of justice and those who would be judges, this is especially important, as they should not be making their decisions based on emotional attachment or emotionally charged pleas, but rather through logic and a sensitivity to the Spirit.

"Prudent:" Prudence, which is alternately translated as "sound mind" or "self controlled," goes well with the idea of temperance. Essentially, not only is the person required to be in control of his temper and emotional swings, but of his actions and speech as well. We want people who are not controlled by their whims or their circumstances, but who are in control of themselves and are able to rise above that which is going on around them.

"Respectable:" Next we seek someone who has a level of respectability in his life. For congregations and individuals to be willing to not only follow, but at times obey these people when the decisions are not the most palatable, the elder has to command respect from those around him. Respect can never be demanded or forced, not in a healthy way at least. Respect must always be earned, and the process and qualities which lead to that earning of respect are essential characteristics in the makeup of a suitable elder.

"Hospitable:" Hospitality is something which is sadly lacking in many Western countries and cultures, but Paul includes it in the list of essential traits. There is good reason for this. It is easy to love those you know, and thus care for them at an appropriate level; however, hospitality often means dealing with people from outside your community and treating them like those you know, opening home and resources up to virtual strangers, making them feel as though they belong.

I once met a rabbi in Israel who invited me to stay at his home for a couple of days. I asked him where I should wait should he not be home when I arrived; he replied that the couch would work. When I looked somewhat dumbfounded by the answer, he replied that he never locked his door because "God forbid that a Jew need a place to sit, a bed to sleep, and I not be there to let them in."

"Able to teach:" Paul required that elders be capable of teaching. As those attempting to lead others in righteousness and holiness, this would only make sense that they not only be able to enforce it but also to teach it. Rabbinically, even today an elder is required to have a student or disciple. This is important for the sake of reproduction of the ministry. If you have the best elder in the world, but he is unable or unwilling to raise up another to take his place, it will end after a single generation. Elders are called to be the highest level of spiritual fathers in congregations, cities, and nations. The only way to become a father is to reproduce.

"Not addicted to wine:" I will sidestep the debate over whether or not a believer should partake of alcoholic beverages and get straight to the matter of addiction. In truth, the issue of addiction itself is divorced from the primary issue of holiness, which comes from possible usage. With addiction, we are talking about control. One who is addicted to alcohol has ceded control over to an outside substance. I believe the primary concern that

Paul has in regard to addiction to wine is not so much a matter of holiness, but more a matter of who or what has control over the prospective elder's life. Once a person cedes that level of control over to anything, Christ is no longer completely his master. The end result is problematic for someone who would rule over God's people in such a position of authority. Every Christian should strive to have no master in their lives but Christ—an elder all the more so.

"Not pugnacious but gentle, uncontentious:" I am combining these two because I believe they essentially represent the same quality. We are instructed here to find a person who is not looking for a fight, who does not like to argue, but rather is meek and a peacemaker. Jesus instructed:

> **"Blessed are the meek, for they will inherit the earth.**

> **"Blessed are those who hunger and thirst for righteousness, for they will be filled.**

> **"Blessed are the merciful, for they will be shown mercy.**

> **"Blessed are the pure in heart, for they will see God.**

> **"Blessed are the peacemakers, for they will be called sons of God" (Matthew 5:5-9 NIV).**

Again these are ideals which every Jesus follower should strive to live up to; however, for one who would seek to walk at this level of authority in the kingdom of God, these are required to be a part of their lives.

"Free from the love of money:" Let us distinguish the difference between wanting adequate finances and loving money. Appreciation for wealth is not the love of money; it is when accruing wealth becomes an end unto itself that it becomes the love of money. About which it is written, **"For the love of money is a root of all kinds of evil. Some people, eager for money, have wandered from the faith and pierced themselves with many griefs"** (I Timothy 6:10 NIV).

There is also the concern that this love of money will lead to a lust for money as it is written, **"Whoever loves money never has money enough; whoever loves wealth is never satisfied with his income"** (see Ecclesiastes 5:10 NIV). Thus there is the concern that one would abuse his privilege as an elder to seek money. Paul also gives in this list those not **"fond of sordid gain"** (see I Timothy 3:8).

The Greek here lends itself to a meaning of money not necessarily gained through immoral dealings such as open theft, but rather through more subtly dishonest practices such as price gouging and the like. Essentially, greed is the driving force behind the motivation and means of making money in this way.

"Able to raise children:" Of all of the required attributes, this one should be the most obvious. Simply put, an elder holds the highest level of authority over the children of God that any human can. These are the people who directly bear the responsibility for the care and upbringing of God's own children. If they are incapable of raising their own children well, how can they be expected to adequately see to God's children?

The Greek Orthodox Church has a profound revelation of this. When they ordain a minister, they take a piece of the communion loaf, the body, and place it into the minister's hand and state, "Guard this sacred trust until the second coming of our Lord at which time He will demand it back from you with an accounting." Jesus Himself said, **"And whoever receives one such child in My name receives Me; but whoever causes one of these little ones who believe in Me to stumble, it would be better for him to have a heavy millstone hung around his neck, and to be drowned in the depth of the sea"** **(Matthew 18:5-6)**. Obviously, God takes His children very seriously, just as any responsible parent would, and thus He expects those who take it upon themselves or who are appointed to care for them have the ability and perform the task to their utmost.

"Not a new convert:" This is probably the most straightforward stipulation of this entire list. Being a father requires a certain level of maturity, and being a father of fathers requires even more. The maturity factor is only one area of concern. However, Paul also states regarding this stipulation, **"lest he become conceited and fall into the condemnation incurred by the devil"** (**see I Timothy 3:6**). As a new convert, even the most mature new believer, the most spiritually adept, are still at risk of falling into the trap of conceit. Pride is a trap which ensnares the most anointed and dedicated of believers. I have often heard Rick Joyner state that when read in chronological order, Paul initially says of himself, **"For I consider myself not in the least inferior to the most eminent apostles"** (**II Corinthians 11:5**). Then as he matures he eventually says of himself, **"It is a trustworthy statement, deserving full acceptance, that Christ Jesus came into the world to save sinners, among whom I am foremost of all"** (**I Timothy 1:15**). If even the Apostle Paul, after being converted by Christ Himself, and after all of his preparation first within the Jewish rabbinic system and then in the desert, would still initially be prideful enough to consider himself equal to the greatest of the apostles, how much more a new believer appointed to a position of such authority as to be above all other levels of church leadership save other elders?

"Have a good name outside the church:" It is not enough to have a good name and respectability within the church; the prospective elder must also be able to command respect from the community. Essentially, the elder has to be one who acts with as much integrity toward the heathen as he does toward the brethren. Proverbs 22:1 says: **"A good name is to be more desired than great wealth."** The value of a good name for every believer cannot be overstated. However, as an elder, we again demand those attributes which we simply encourage among the flock. The reasons are numerous, but chief among them is that the kingdom of God is here to conquer the kingdoms of this world, not through carnal weapons but with spiritual. As the earthly leaders of the kingdom, the elders of the body of Christ should have such a reputation for honesty, integrity, and the ability at governance that the world will beat a path to the door of the church to learn how to govern the secular and passing kingdoms of this world.

"Not double-tongued:" Along with a good name and reputation also comes honesty. Being double-tongued simply means saying one thing and doing another, or telling one person one thing and another person something different. To put it simply, to be double-tongued is to be a liar. **"Truthful lips will be established forever, but a lying tongue is only for a moment" (Proverbs 12:19).** The government that we attempt to establish through the church should be built to last forever. Our goal should be to accomplish as much of the final redemption as possible—to build a kingdom in this world so when our King returns He will feel at home. In order to do this, it has to be built on a foundation that God is willing to establish for eternity. Part of that foundation has to be truth and honesty.

The Spiritual Authority of Elders

These requirements are weighty and serious. Let me state that this is not a drift to legalism nor is it the place for a full discussion of law and legalism (see Chapter Seven). In short, the definition of legalism is requiring obedience to rules for salvation or right standing with God, thus replacing the perfect work of the cross with a substitute of our works. These requirements have nothing to do with salvation or right standing with God, nor do they set aside the work of the cross. There are no draftees in church leadership, especially when it comes to the eldership. At this level, they are all volunteers. In other words, if you do not like the package, do not sign on. The requirements are to protect the leadership and the flock. Eldership, as I will demonstrate in a moment, which comes with a great deal of authority and power, also comes with great responsibility.

Let us now turn to examining the authority of elders. Matthew 18:18-19 states, **"Truly I say to you, whatever you shall bind on earth shall be bound in heaven; and whatever you loose on earth shall be loosed in heaven. Again I say to you, that if two of you agree on earth about anything that they may ask, it shall be done for them by My Father who is in heaven."** The terms "bind" and "loose" are Jewish legal language. The primary work that one has to learn in order to become a rabbi is called *Issur V'Heter,* translated "bound and loosed." In Judaism, even in the Judaism of Jesus' day, to bind something meant to forbid it, and to loose something meant to permit it. Often in the church, we have looked at this passage completely in a spiritual light; however, I believe a more accurate reading would be to see this as an investiture of governmental power within the body of Christ.

One of the key principles of biblical interpretation is juxtaposition. In this, you look at the Scripture immediately surrounding the passage that you are examining as a means of interpretation. It is interesting that this passage on binding and loosing comes immediately after a discussion of how justice should be administered within the church. Any first-century Jewish reader, and many of the early Christians as they were fairly intimate with synagogue life, upon reading this section of Matthew would immediately see that Jesus was talking about first establishing a proper chain of events and evidence leading into a religious court. In the very next line, they would see that Jesus was investing His chosen leadership with authority that was not only to be honored on earth, but would be honored in heaven as well.

The idea of binding and loosing also empowers the eldership with the ability to establish doctrine and practice within their respective communities. This is not to say that they gain any type of infallibility in their doctrine or teaching, or the traditions which they set for their communities. However, it does grant a level of trust, which unless biblical evidence can be demonstrated showing the fallacy, we trust that these things are intended for our good and are worthwhile. This can be seen most especially in the life of Martin Luther. Luther had no intention of breaking away from the historical eldership of the church as it was then, or of rejecting its doctrines and traditions in their entirety. Rather, Luther's desire was to bring correction and open discussion about areas of doctrine and tradition which he perceived, and rightly in my opinion, to have deviated from the pure teaching of Scripture.

All of this is not to say that Jesus was not also investing the church, and most especially her eldership, with spiritual authority. Quite the contrary, Jesus invested the church and her eldership with more spiritual authority than many today realize. I believe the New Covenant surpasses the Old Covenant in every way, and the authority granted our elders under the New Covenant also surpasses that of the elders of the Old Covenant. However, many elders today are not even living up to the authority granted under the Old Covenant. So I am going to turn there for a while and demonstrate the authority that God gave to eldership under the Old Covenant and how it manifests itself.

One of the greatest examples of eldership authority comes in Deuteronomy 21:1-8:

> If a slain person is found lying in the open country in the land which the LORD your God gives you to possess, and it is not known who has struck him,

> then your elders and your judges shall go out and measure the distance to the cities which are around the slain one.

> And it shall be that the city which is nearest to the slain man, that is, the elders of that city, shall take a heifer of the herd, which has not been worked and which has not pulled in a yoke;

> and the elders of that city shall bring the heifer down to a valley with running water, which has not been plowed or sown, and shall break the heifer's neck there in the valley.

> Then the priests, the sons of Levi, shall come near, for the LORD your God has chosen them to serve Him and to bless in the name of the LORD; and every dispute and every assault shall be settled by them.

> And all the elders of that city which is nearest to the slain man shall wash their hands over the heifer whose neck was broken in the valley;

and they shall answer and say, "Our hands have not shed this blood, nor did our eyes see it.

"Forgive Thy people Israel whom Thou hast redeemed, O LORD, and do not place the guilt of innocent blood in the midst of Thy people Israel." And the bloodguiltiness shall be forgiven them.

This passage raises a question: Why were the elders held accountable for something that did not even happen in their city?

In the days of the Old Testament, there were no suburbs, so the cities were responsible for the lands around them. Still, we need to ask, why the elders? The rabbis' comment on this is that because the elders hold spiritual authority over and thus responsibility for their cities and the land around them, then that land is the responsibility of the city. Elders in the Old Testament sat in the gates as judges, not just to settle disputes, but to guard over the influences that came into their cities. According to the commentaries, they were not simply responsible for physical influences but also the spiritual influences. The rabbis believed that the elders, through their righteous living and intercession, could control the spiritual influences within their cities. Thus for someone to come up murdered and no one to know who did it, the responsibility fell back on the elders. The reason being if they had pursued their intercession to the extent that they should have, such a tragedy would not have happened. The reasoning behind this answer is quite simple and straightforward in its logic: God does not assign responsibility where He has not already given authority.

What this is essentially saying is that as an elder, or more appropriately a body of elders, the spiritual leadership of a city has the ability to state what spiritual influences will have a foothold within their cities. Biblically, the elders have the ability to state with authority, "Not in my town!" and the powers and principalities have to obey. The simple reason is as God holds them accountable, they have the ability to say no. This authority extends into every area. In the beginning of this chapter, I referred to Mr. Bannister and spoke of his record-breaking sub-four-minute mile. Before he broke the record, no one thought it was possible, but within weeks of him breaking that record, others did it repeatedly. Therefore, I am going to bring modern examples of elders putting this authority to good use in the hope that it will inspire the body to take up the call.

In the past century, a demonic empire known as the Nazis arose in Europe and quickly began to conquer much of their hemisphere. The Nazis also had a penchant for executing Jews. In 1942, Rommel was driving across North Africa and seemed virtually unstoppable. By this point, the world was aware of what the Nazis were doing with the Jews, and North Africa and the Middle East actually had larger Jewish populations than did Europe, and thus the risk was great. Two great rabbis, Yisrael Abuchatzeirah and Yehudah Fatyah, managed to requisition a plane from the British high command. They took this plane up over the El Almein battlefield, and began to repent for the sins of their generation and for allowing such a demonic influence to enter the world. Then they pronounced judgment on the Nazi forces—Rommel in particular, and declared that he would not win another battle. The next day at the battle of El Almein, Rommel suffered his first defeat in what would become an unending string of defeats that drove him out of Africa and all the way back to Germany. This entire story was published in the August 1987 edition of the *Jerusalem Post Magazine*.

In another instance during World War II, the Bulgarian Regime of King Boris III actively supported the deportation of the Jews from Bulgaria. Into this came the two primary leaders of the Bulgarian Church, Metropolitan Stephen of Sophia and Metropolitan Kiril. These men became convinced that the Nazi regime was driven by a demonic force and thus called an ecumenical council within Bulgaria to decide this issue. The council decreed that the deportation of Jews was ungodly and that it should be opposed by both prayer and action. On February 22, 1943, Bulgaria signed a top secret agreement with Nazi Germany: Twenty thousand Jews from both Bulgaria and its occupied territories were to be deported to death camps in Poland. Through a series of events which can only be called miraculous, this leaked to the church leadership. The Metropolitans assembled their bishops who then assembled their priests who assembled their flocks and brought them to stand between the Nazis and the Jews about to be herded onto cattle cars. Kiril lay down across the tracks before the train. Stephen stood against the Gestapo Commandant and told him that if he intended to take the Jews, he would have to take all of these Bulgarians with him, and the Bulgarians would not go without a fight. In a radical shift that itself is miraculous, the Nazis backed down, and not a single Jew was deported from Bulgaria.

Both of these instances where God's leadership stood up are documented history. They used the authority God had given His leadership under the Old Covenant and triumphed spectacularly over a demonically-controlled nation. Despite the fact that the Nazi regime was at the height of its power during both of these instances, they were defenseless to stand against the spiritual power that was released against them by God's faithful. Again, this is a level of authority given in the Old Covenant. We are no longer under the Old Covenant, but under the New Covenant. We have a better covenant with better promises (see Hebrews 8:6). If the Old Covenant offered authority over spiritual and secular powers that opposed the purposes of God, how much more so the New Covenant?

I cannot help but wonder about the power and authority, which many of us have not even begun to pursue. The world we live in is a messed up place. We are confronted with disease, immorality, abortion, and many other issues that need to be confronted and stopped. If the leadership of the Old Covenant had authority over those things when they attempted to come into their cities and were expected to be able to put a stop to them, how much more so is the leadership of the church under the New Covenant?

If a couple of rabbis, sixty years ago, who had no relationship with Jesus, could call upon the authority granted under the Old Covenant to put a stop to the devastation caused by the Nazi regime in their land, how much more should the leadership of the body of Christ who have a living and real relationship with the God of all? I believe that we are in a time when the Lord Jesus Christ will raise up an eldership who will stand in this authority to kick sin out of their lands and bring the righteousness of the King in.

I would be remiss, however, if I also did not bring one final point. All of this power and authority also comes with a higher level of responsibility and accountability. Paul writes in I Timothy 5:19-20, **"Do not receive an accusation against an elder except on the basis of two or three witnesses. Those who continue in sin, rebuke in the presence of all, so that the rest also may be fearful of sinning."**

It is important to note that any other time in the New Testament when we see a brother found in a trespass, it is commanded to be kept quiet. Usually we are not supposed to bring the faults of our brethren to light, but rather deal with them in a spirit of love and correction, while protecting the brother from embarrassment. When dealing with an elder this is not the case. One who walks in such authority and who sits in judgment of others is called to live at a higher standard, and when they fall, their fall is made public, according to Paul, so that others will not fall into the same trespass but live in the fear of sin.

This is not an easy place in which to live, and this responsibility should not be taken lightly. When all things are considered, I understand why so many are reluctant to step up to this level of authority. However, at the same time the words of Rabban Gamaliel, the teacher of the Apostle Paul come to my mind: "If not me then who; if not now, when?" I believe the Lord is asking us that very question in regard to this issue. If we will not step up and take this on, then who will? If now is not the time, will there ever be a good time? I do not believe that we can let too many more generations pass without the power and authority of the church leadership. As our world sinks further into hurt, pain, and depravity, we need an eldership who can stand up and draw a line in the Spirit and put an end to it. However, first someone has to step up and go for it.

CHAPTER SIX
DISCIPLESHIP

E VEN IF WE HAVE THE BEST ELDERS IN the world, men of such spiritual stature and authority as has not been seen for a millennia, it will all be for nothing if they do not reproduce. A single generation is not enough. Even if we raise up from our midst those that will carry this banner today—if there are none ready to do so tomorrow, we leave the body of Christ in no better shape than it is now, perhaps even worse.

The historical record easily shows why the church long ago abandoned a system of justice. The reason was that it had failed in its midst. Those like John Calvin tried to revive it. His efforts in Geneva were immense; however, they also led him to be exiled from that city more than once. The reasons for his failure were his excesses. Often he would push the bounds far into legalism to the point that the city would rebel in search of liberty, only then to fall to license. The persecution of the Anabaptists (the predominant foundation of

America's Christianity), as well as others he deemed to be theologically deviant, were an inherent part in Calvin's system of justice. His reformed theocracy was for the most part a rebirth of many of the extremes that the reformers wanted to escape in Catholicism.

The damage done to true biblical justice is immeasurable; the effects of those failures are still felt today. Even now many within the church fear a return to church-run justice because they fear a descent into the problems of before. If we raise up only a single generation of elders and justice within our midst, far from helping the church, we will add to the weight of evidence that says she should stay out of it.

This is not meant at all to be a discouragement. Rather, I wish to clearly illuminate the path we are taking and its possible pitfalls so they may be avoided. Many great ministries have passed from this earth without having adequately reproduced themselves, and the body of Christ has suffered for it. Imagine if a person like Smith Wigglesworth had reproduced himself in just twelve people, following the example of the Lord, then if those twelve into twelve more, and so forth. There would be no lack of the miraculous in the Western church—that is certain. Sadly, we can only imagine. This is not a situation that I want to see continue in any branch of the ministry, but it is definitely one that I want to address as we look to reestablishing a ministry that has so long been absent from the church. The only cure I believe is discipleship on a radical level.

Discipleship is the primary way that God has given to train each generation of believers and leaders. Regrettably, many of us do not have a good concept of what discipleship is. Some are even scared of the concept on account of past abuses. From the time of Moses, discipleship was an essential element in the training of subsequent generations and was also a key element of the commission which Jesus gave His own disciples before sending them out into the world: **"And Jesus came up and spoke to them, saying, 'All authority has been given to Me in heaven and on earth. Go therefore and make disciples of all the nations, baptizing them in the name of the Father and the Son and the Holy Spirit, teaching them to observe all that I commanded you; and lo, I am with you always, even to the end of the age'"** (Matthew 28:18-20). I would like to propose that perhaps the time has come to for us to once again look to this element of the gospel, and to once again claim it for the body of Christ.

As I have already said, discipleship has been an essential part of training leadership from the time of Moses. Today, within the Jewish world, this discipleship has become highly developed and greatly systematized. Despite all of that, it has not lost its essential character. It still remains one generation training the next, to the best of its ability. One of the scriptural derivations is Numbers 8:24-25: **"This is what applies to the Levites: from twenty-five years old and upward they shall enter to perform service in the work of the tent of meeting. But at the age of fifty years they shall retire from service in the work and not work any more."**

There are several points that the rabbis find of interest in this single verse. We have already learned in Exodus 30 that all people are eligible for service from the age of twenty. Now we find that the Levites do not actually enter the service of temple until they are twenty-five. We must ask what happens in those intermediate years, from ages twenty until twenty-five. All of the rabbinic commentators agree that they are being trained and discipled for the positions that they will hold.

There are several interesting points to this. First, most children in ancient Israelite culture began training in their trade (what they did for a living) from the time they were thirteen. As the Levites were specifically forbidden from holding any other positions, this additional training came after what others had already received. For instance, to be a carpenter, training would occur for seven years, from the ages of thirteen to twenty. To be a Levite, at twenty, there would be another five years of training. This is interesting, considering the actual duties of the Levites. The most famous of the Levitical duties is of course the temple orchestra and choir. However, these were the least of their duties as far as time is concerned. In regards to the worship in the temple, the Levites were broken up into twenty-four clans, which were then subdivided into twenty-four courses. Each clan would serve one week every six months; each course would serve for one hour a day. Adding this up, the Levites only served as the musicians for about fourteen hours a year.

The majority of their duties revolved around the upkeep of the temple. That is a very polite way of saying they were the janitors. They swept floors, cleaning the many messes that happened. They also served as ushers, receiving the offering and ensuring that the people found their way into the courts. Besides my own amusement that God mated worship with scrubbing toilets, I find it even more interesting that He required twelve years of total training before a Levite could pick up either a guitar or a toilet brush within the temple. Then they actually only served for a total of twenty-five years, which is almost one year of training for every two years of service.

One has to ask: What happened to those Levites who were above fifty? We know that even after their service was completed, the now retired Levites still received their portion of the offerings, thus they were still supported and fed by the temple. We also know that God has a general rule: **"If a man will not work, he shall not eat" (see II Thessalonians 3:10** NIV**).** It is well-established that the portion the Levites received was in return for their service in the temple. Their service now was training the next generation. It was not those who were currently in the ministry that were the primary brain trust training the future Levites; it was those whose time had already passed—those who had successfully served the Lord for many years were chosen to train those whose time was yet to come.

Too often this is not the case. Often the elderly amongst the ranks of the ministry are considered to be irrelevant, and thus relegated to minister to other seniors or some small and dying congregation or to retirement. In truth, none of those options were ever God's plan. God's plan was to use them—to have them pour their lives into the next generation. I once had a friend who was active in the ministry ask me about discipleship in the Jewish world. When I laid it out for him, he said simply that it sounds great, but they just did not have time. That is the way it should be. Those actively involved in the work really should not be the ones doing the primary training. Jesus told His own disciples, **"The harvest is plentiful, but the workers are few. Therefore beseech the Lord of the harvest to send out workers into His harvest" (see Matthew 9:37-38).** Those gathering the wheat need not be distracted by teaching others how to make sheaves. Rather, this is the place for those who have already run their race.

Look at the Lord's own example with the Levites: twelve years of training and twenty-five years of faithful service before they were ready to do the main work of instructing others in the service. The point here is not to get caught up on some kind of legalistic requirement for people who want to disciple others or for people to enter ministry, rather to suggest that instead of putting those best-suited to discipling others out to pasture, making use of them. Personally, I believe that the church and the world would be amazed at the leaders the church would turn out if she began to allow those who have walked faithfully for many years to pour their lives into the next generation.

I believe with all of my heart that the many great things that people say about the Jewish people, and the brilliance of their rabbis especially, is best attributed to this one factor. Whatever good the Jewish people have achieved did not happen overnight; it has taken thousands of years of one generation pouring into another, constantly pushing the limits and striving for higher and higher levels in both education and spirituality to make the Jewish people today what they are. We can only imagine where the church would be today if her great leaders throughout history did the same. However, I do not believe that it will take thousands of years or hundreds of generations to reach much higher levels. By the grace of the New Covenant and the guidance of the Holy Spirit, I believe that the church could achieve in one generation what would take the world hundreds.

To date, the great majority of the body of Christ seems to look at discipleship as a process for new believers; thus the majority of resources that can be found focus primarily on that target audience. In my own research, the best that I have found are organizations and resources to take a new believer to the level of a home group leader. While any attempt to bring Christians to a higher level of maturity is admirable, it is still a long way from the goal. A passage of Scripture that I believe best sums up the idea of discipleship is Ephesians 4:11-13: **"And He gave some as apostles, and some as prophets, and some as evangelists, and some as pastors and teachers, for the equipping of the saints for the work of service, to the building up of the body of Christ; until we all attain to the unity of the faith, and of the knowledge of the Son of God, to a mature man, to the measure of the stature which belongs to the fullness of Christ."**

I believe that this passage speaks of taking believers to much higher levels of maturity than simply the basics of the faith and possibly even home group leaders. I believe it calls us to bring people to the level of being accurate representatives of Christ in the world. Perhaps if we become radically committed to discipleship, we will redefine the level of spiritual authority and maturity in the average home group leader.

If we were truly living the level of discipleship to which the church is called, we would be bringing new believers and even old believers much further than even congregational leadership roles. We would be making internationally recognized evangelists and ministries. As a modern example, consider Billy Graham. Without question, he has a stunning track record for faithful ministry to the body of Christ and the world. However, as he now finishes his race, or at least that leg of his race, where are those that he has raised up to carry the banner forward? The vacuum that is left when a great leader of the body such as Billy Graham steps down from active ministry can at times take generations to fill once again. The Jewish people still weep and mourn the loss of the many great luminaries amongst their own leadership in the last century. Our hearts break when we imagine the light, truth, and wisdom that were robbed from us by wicked men in the Holocaust and Stalinist Russia. For sixty years we have been rebuilding—to the point where only now do the leaders of the generation feel that we are beginning to equal what was lost so that we may move forward.

As members of the body of Christ, we should be crushed to think of the great spiritual fathers and mothers of the last one hundred years that we put out to pasture and ignored—that they went to their graves without pouring their light, wisdom, and experience into another generation. Let us not lose another one hundred years.

CHAPTER SEVEN

JUSTICE, LAW, AND LEGALISM

I N DISCUSSING THE SUBJECT OF JUSTICE within the body of Christ, I have had numerous people say that it is not justice they want, but grace. I have even had a few people ask me directly to help them find biblical evidence that justice is the opposite of God's grace. This speaks of a profound misunderstanding of what justice is. Somewhere over the course of time, since the reformation, some have overreacted so much to the problem of legalism that they now look upon any form of law or guiding principle as the opposite of God's intent. I hope to be able to demonstrate here that a proper understanding of justice is as important as an understanding of grace.

The Scripture states, **"Righteousness and justice are the foundation of Your throne"** (see Psalm 89:14). To start from the beginning, we have to look into what a throne is and why it matters where God sits. In Jewish tradition and thought, the throne of God symbolizes God's interaction with the world and His people. You will notice that in the inaugural visions of the major prophets—Isaiah, Jeremiah, and Ezekiel—as well as in the Book of Revelation, each of the interactive visions start with a throne vision. To give imagery in ancient times, when a king would receive people, even his dearest friends, he would come out and sit on his throne. That being the case, for God to have full involvement with His people, righteousness and justice must be present.

A throne is also a symbol of leadership. The throne is the symbol of authority that a king holds. If God is to be our King, He must have a throne upon which to sit. He must have a place of authority within our midst. However, if we cut justice out of the mix, we undermine that place of authority. The foundation of the throne can be compared to the legs of a chair—if you take two legs from any chair, it is impossible to sit in it. To the extent we remove either righteousness or justice from our lives and from our communities, in equal proportion we will undermine and destroy the foundation of our relationship with God. To that extent, we will remove from our midst a place suitable to the Lord. God cannot be the King of our hearts and our lives if He cannot sit upon the throne of His rule because we have knocked the foundation out from under it.

Not only is it necessary for both righteousness and justice to be present in order for there to be a proper foundation, but in truth we cannot have one without the other. Righteousness and justice are in fact two different sides to the same coin. Without justice, there is no standard by which we can measure righteousness. There is nothing to tell us when we have gone off the path of proper living. At the same time, without righteousness all justice will ultimately be perverted. It does not matter how perfect the system is; if the people behind it are hedonistic sinners, it will be a perverted system serving their wants and lusts. One need only look to Jesus' trial to see this. I have no doubt that the system of justice which God commanded Israel, and carries through into the New Testament, was a perfect system. However, when wicked men hijacked it, they perverted that perfect system to the point where they actually put its Creator on the cross.

We must define what justice is. We can throw around terms, but if we each still have our own preconceived notions of what something means, it does not help with understanding. On a very basic level, a system of justice in any secular government is primarily in place to protect the rights and privileges of its citizens. In the kingdom of God, justice is also supposed to be a protection of the rights of the citizenry. The purpose of justice within the kingdom is to ensure that each child of God receives every right and ounce of benefit for which the Lord Jesus Christ died. In order to accomplish this, the system of justice in the kingdom, much like in our secular justice systems, is supposed to set the law, standard of living, and relation to one another.

The word "law" in the previous sentence is not an error, nor is it a typo; the intent was to say it just the way it reads. Law is a part of justice. Law is necessary for life; without law there is not a standard by which we live. Most importantly though, law does not equal legalism; law and legalism are not the same thing. For instance, on every blow-dryer there is a label stating quite explicitly not to use that blow-dryer while taking a bath. We look at such labels as commonsense, but if it were commonsense, they would not need to put it there. Disobeying the label does not necessarily affect your relationship with the Lord. It may qualify you for a Darwin award; it may even bring you into a literal face-to-face relationship with God; but in truth, the law is there to warn you about the consequences of inappropriate behavior. I personally do not know of anyone who reads one of those restrictions on a blow-dryer and then complains that the company who made it is being legalistic.

The same can be said of DUI (driving under the influence) laws which each state and country have enacted. These laws are there for the protection of every citizen. If a person is impaired, driving a vehicle simply is not safe. If not stopped, those who do so, in many cases, end up hurting or killing an innocent person. Again, when most people read or hear about the DUI laws of their locality, they do not complain that their state is being legalistic—most quietly thank God that someone has had the good sense to watch over the safety of the general public. There are those who do complain, but in my experience most of them live in a state of lawlessness which disregards those around them for the sake of their own pleasures. I will write more about this in a moment, but for now I want to stay concentrated on the idea that law is not legalism.

Law, taken within the proper context, is a system of guidelines which enables us to love God and our neighbors in a way that will not damage them or us. There is a story in the Talmud[24] that depicts this dichotomy between law and legalism well. A pagan became interested in Judaism, so he went to a great rabbi named Shammai[25] and said, "Teach me the entire law while standing on one foot." Shammai grew angry and said it was impossible—there are 613 commandments in the Torah[26] and each must be learned and mastered with all of its derivations before one can begin to understand and live the law. So the pagan went away. Eventually, this same pagan came to Hillel[27] and made the same request of him. Hillel without hesitating stood on one

---

24   Shabbat 31a
25   One of the two greatest rabbis of his generation.
26   There are, when counted, 613 specific commandments throughout the five books of Moses that God specifically commanded Israel. Then from the beginning of the rabbinic period in Nehemiah's time, the rabbis began to interpret and explain each of these commandments and their specific applications. This interpretation eventually turned into the Talmud, a 30,000 page document.
27   The other great rabbi of his generation, as well as the grandfather and one of the two teachers of Gamaliel, Paul's teacher.

foot and said, "'And you shall love the LORD your God with all your heart and with all your soul and with all your might' (Deuteronomy 6:5), and 'you shall love your neighbor as yourself,' (see Leviticus 19:18); the rest is commentary; go and learn." On account of this answer, the pagan was converted to Judaism.

This is the prime difference between a proper relationship with and understanding of law and legalism. Law in its proper context gives us an understanding of how to either love and serve God or how to love and properly treat your neighbor. Thus was Hillel able to say that the other 611 commandments were nothing more than commentary on these two. To Shammai, the legalist, this was not good enough. For him, the law was not a means to an end, but both the means and the end. For him, the law had become an idol that so consumed him that he allowed it to block others from coming into a loving relationship with God. While law creates healthy boundaries that enable relationships, legalism causes distance which disables relationships.

Within legalism there is no room for love or for forgiveness. Legalism requires strict adherence to the rules and the imputation of guilt for the slightest infraction. The Book of Hebrews 9:8-10 states: **"The Holy Spirit is signifying this, that the way into the holy place has not yet been disclosed, while the outer tabernacle is still standing, which is a symbol for the** present time. Accordingly both gifts and sacrifices are offered which cannot make the worshiper perfect in conscience, since they relate only to food and drink and various washings, regulations for the body imposed until a time of reformation." Notice the passage does not say that these sacrifices are unable to make a person right in the eyes of God, but within their own minds and consciences they still feel their guilt. The reason for this is not the imperfection of the system which God laid down, but rather it is the rational end of a system which descended into legalism. Once legalism was allowed in the door, simple items of food, some spilled wine, or a dip in mikvah[28] is not capable of rectifying the breaking of a commandment because it cannot undo that which has been done. Legalism does not allow for forgiveness and grace. Even though the Law which God laid down makes provision for His forgiveness and grace to minister to the human lost condition, legalism excised it out.

It is important to note that just because we have faith in Jesus Christ, this does not make us free from legalism. I was once attending an inner healing class put on by a fairly famous inner healing ministry. They were lecturing on helping people get forgiveness for past, unrepented sins, and in this process they spoke about theft. The leader of this organization made a statement that God could not forgive a person until they had made

---

28   A type of Jewish baptismal used for cleansing impurity.

restitution, even if the sin was committed before the person was a Christian. I did not take this well and made quite a vocal protest. Essentially, I felt then and still believe now they were stating that the blood of Christ was insufficient to cover that sin. This person and others there made the point that I was a rabbi and thus should be in full favor of this. My reply was simple; early on in the rediscovery of my Jewish roots, I descended into legalism, and while free of it now, as a repentant legalist I am familiar with that spirit—we can smell our own. Legalism will always take law and make it a thing that must be done in order to be acceptable to God instead of what should be done to please God.

Legalism promotes idolization of law but prevents and blocks wholesome and healthy relationships. Law on the other hand, when used as a means with a spirit of love, creates healthy boundaries which lead to healthy relationships. For instance, in my marriage there are rules—laws, if you will—that guide the way my wife and I relate to one another. Some of these rules are things such as we do not seek romantic relationships with other people. We do not strike one another. We speak and treat each other with respect. These rules should be a part of every marriage relationship. Again, healthy individuals would not see these as legalistic rules, but good advice for a lasting marriage. Far from locking us into a system of death that blocks a true relationship of love and trust from developing, these rules establish the necessary healthy boundaries that ensure not only the development of a loving relationship, but also the continued life and growth of that relationship.

In truth, God's Law works the same way. Paul, the man so often quoted as being anti-law, himself states, **"Therefore the Law has become our tutor to lead us to Christ, that we may be justified by faith" (Galatians 3:24).** Notice the Law is not the end, it is not the goal, but rather it leads us to the goal. Just as maps and road signs help us plan a trip and stay on the proper route by pointing us in the right direction, so too is the purpose of the Law. We do not go on a road trip for the sake of the map or the road signs—we go on a road trip for the purpose of reaching a certain destination. So, too, our purpose in life should be to grow closer to the Lord and to grow in love. God's commandments, His Law, are not the purpose for the journey, but they are the map and signs along the way that let us know that we are still upon the proper path and headed in the right direction. Just as the signs are the means and not the end, so the Law has to be the means and never the end.

This idea is even evidenced within the order of events in Scripture. Most commonly, when we think of Law, we think of the Torah that God gave the Israelites through Moses. The interesting thing is that the covenant was not based upon that Law—at least it was not supposed to be. The covenant may have been twisted into legalism, but initially the covenant was supposed to be based on God's redemption in bringing the Jewish people out of Egypt. So much so that when God began giving the Jewish people the Law through the discourse often called the "ten commandments," He stated, **"I am the Lord your God, who brought you out of the land of Egypt, out of the house of slavery"** (**Exodus 20:2**). This was the very first commandment. In fact, the formula **"I am the Lord your God, who brought you out of the land of Egypt"** is used more than 150 times throughout the Torah by God as the reason why the Israelites should obey whatever commandment He is giving them at the time. The point seems to be clear: God is not so much demanding that the people follow commandments as much as He is asking them to respond to the great work He has done on their behalf.

The same is true of the New Covenant. Long before Paul or any other apostle wrote a single letter commanding believers to act according to certain principles, Jesus first laid down His life for man so we could attain perfection in God's sight through His own sacrifice. Only then do we begin to receive the instruction of the New Testament, and even there I would argue that the language is the same.

Paul writes, **"Therefore, I urge you, brothers, in view of God's mercy, to offer your bodies as living sacrifices, holy and pleasing to God—this is your spiritual act of worship" (Romans 12:1 NIV).** Here, too, Paul is telling us not to seek a relationship with God through our deeds, but rather to respond to God's love for us with deeds. By always viewing our works as a response to the incredible goodness of God, we will prevent ourselves from being deceived into thinking that it is through the merit of our deeds that we draw closer to Him. Having laid down His life for us, I do believe that Jesus deserves our very best in return.

Often I have seen the New Testament held up against the Old Testament as grace versus Law. I do not think that God's overall message has changed that much over time. Yes, we do have a better covenant; but a covenant has always been by His grace. Even the New Testament is not devoid of commandments. I had a Jewish friend who was once having a Bible study for a group of Christians. He decided to have them go through the New Testament and list, categorize, and count each commandment given through the New Testament. He called me one day very excited. Apparently, his group had counted over nine hundred individual commandments throughout the New Testament, and he was very happy that "they have more than us." I told him in fairly blunt terms that this was far from the brightest idea he had ever had. However,

119

the point stands: If you want to find a commandment, it can be found even in the New Testament.

This may come as a surprise, but even though I am a rabbi and live by the Mosaic Law myself, I am absolutely not advocating that Christians even think of taking upon themselves the Laws of the Old Covenant. For that matter, I am also absolutely opposed to believers blindly following the rules laid down in the New Testament as an unbending law. Rather, I am advocating the use of the rules laid down in the New Testament to guide us in our relationships with God and with each other.

There were two instances in my life that struck home the difference between legalism and Law to the greatest extent. I was in a synagogue one day and there was a visiting rabbi. During the confessional section of the prayer service, he began uncontrollably weeping. After the service I asked him what was wrong. He told me that once, a couple of years ago, he had drunk a non-kosher drink by accident, and was thus attempting to atone for that accidental transgression—that he was trying to abolish the separation that it caused between him and God.

Compare that to another situation I experienced. I have a friend who is a rabbi. He called me one day saying that he needed some help at his house and would give me no more details over the phone. When I arrived at his house, I could tell that he was rather agitated and more than a little embarrassed, so I asked him what was going on. As it turns out, he and his wife, because of a change of ingredients in a product they used in their kitchen, had been violating one of the major kosher laws for just over a year, and now the kitchen needed to be made kosher again. My mind was brought back to the scene at the synagogue where the man was weeping so bitterly over one small accidental mistake. I could not imagine what the fallout from this would be. So I asked my friend what he was going to do, and his answer set me back as much as the one I had received at the synagogue. He said he needed to get new dishes[29] and try harder not to do it again.

I was quite struck by that statement; in fact, it shocked me as much as the visiting rabbi at the synagogue. To me, the two together gave a good picture of the difference between legalism and Law. To a legalist, there can be no forgiveness, no grace, and no mercy. A violation of a rule drives a wedge into the relationship that cannot be easily removed, and in some cases may never be removed, if only on a subconscious level. However, to one whom the Law is as it was always intended to be, guidelines for righteous living, the answer is simple. Make your apologies and move on—hopefully learning from your own mistakes.

29   Because the old ones were no longer kosher (fitting for Jewish dietary law).

As I thought about this, another realization struck me. Long before God gave Israel the Law at Mount Sinai, He first delivered them from Egypt. His salvation from the house of bondage was not conditional on Israel's keeping His Law, but rather on His grace alone. In the same way, long before a single pen stroke of the New Testament ever made it to paper, Jesus laid down His life to free us all from our spiritual bondage. In both cases, the many writings and rules which may have followed were given to be a response, a way of living uprightly and in appropriate response to the grace and mercy that the Lord of all had already shown those that He chose to be His people.

Legalism implies that we need to do something in order to be acceptable to God—that we need to live in a certain way in order to be brought near to God. Stated simply, that is a denial of the finished work of the cross. Christ, through His death, brought us as close to God as we are ever going to get. All that remains is our own unbelief. It is our unbelief, our inability to acknowledge and accept such love, that brings us to a place where we seek a form of legalism as the answer. If, however, we can set aside our own unbelief and simply accept the love that God has shown us, then we will see the rules for what they truly are, a means of living a life worthy of our calling (see Ephesians 4:1).

Paul writes concerning the Law, **"Love is the fulfillment of the law" (see Romans 13:10 NIV)**. Love sums up God's law; it is just that simple. There is a reason that when Jesus was questioned as to the greatest commandment, **"Jesus answered, "The foremost is, 'Hear, O Israel! The Lord our God is one Lord; and you shall love the Lord your God with all your heart, and with all your soul, and with all your mind, and with all your strength.' "The second is this, 'You shall love your neighbor as yourself.' There is no other commandment greater than these"(Mark 12:29-31)**. If we truly love God and love man and are in perfect relationship, embodying perfect love, rules are unnecessary. Rules are only necessary for those of us (I, the chief amongst them) who have not yet attained to perfect love. Until that love is perfected, rules are necessary to keep us from doing harm to those with whom we have relationship.

Our relationships with God in many ways can be compared to a marriage. The longer I am married to my wife, the more I instinctively know what makes her happy and what will hurt her feelings. Thus, the longer we are married, the more these things become instinctual, and the less I need her to tell me what not to do and what to do. In the same way, God's rules are to help us from hurting God's heart and from hurting those around us. The longer we are in relationship with Him, the less we will need to have those things spelled out for us.

One of the things which justice does in God's system is to help enforce these rules, especially between the brethren, thus ensuring that should love fail, the children of God would be protected from those who would do them harm. Also, it is a means to heal those relationships which may have been harmed on account of such a failing. It is this upholding of the rules that God has laid down for relationships between the brethren and with other people for which justice is best known. However, justice is far more than law; it is much more than enforcing rules or regulations. In its proper context, justice also means loving our neighbors, here and abroad.

Chapter Eight
The Heart of Justice

THERE DEFINITELY IS A STRONG RELATION-
ship between law and justice, and I believe it is one
of the reasons why the body of Christ has been seemingly
so afraid to enter into a system of justice. Having hopefully
made the law aspect of justice much more appealing, it
is now to be demonstrated that law is only one aspect of
justice. In truth, there is much more to justice than law.
Justice in its proper context is a means by which we can
love our neighbors, locally and abroad.

The prophet Isaiah says, **"Seek justice, encourage
the oppressed, defend the cause of the fatherless,
plead the case of the widow" (see Isaiah 1:17 NIV).**
Right after the prophet exhorts the people to **"seek
justice,"** he tells them to **"encourage the oppressed."**
Encouraging the oppressed is in fact as much an
aspect of justice as the upholding of any rules. It is
important to understand that in a secular government
justice exists only to uphold the rights of the citizenry,
so, too, in God's kingdom justice serves to uphold the

rights of the citizenry. Reaching out to those living in poverty, the homeless, and the persecuted church are all aspects of justice.

One way to look at this aspect of justice is to consider the way you would feel if one of your own children was in trouble and someone helped him. If your child was homeless, living in poverty, starving, or in some other way in desperate need of help, how would you feel toward an individual who selflessly helped them? Most likely the benefactor would be your new best friend. The truth is that while the church as a whole is the bride, the individuals are God's children. The homeless people living in our cities, the impoverished in our nation, the starving and persecuted around the world are also God's children. If we who are wicked would so love someone who helped one of our own children, it stands to reason that God, who is perfectly good, would only respond similarly to us. Justice then is not simply a legal system, but rather a means by which we can stand with God on behalf of His children against those who would seek their harm. True justice, godly justice, seeks not to punish, but to heal.

A story that brought home to me how seriously God looks on all of this was told by the son of the Chofetz Chaim. The story was about a butcher named Dobbie who rented a house to a widow and her orphaned son. One winter the widow was incapable of paying the rent one month, so Dobbie simply pushed the thatched roof in and evicted them, sending them into the streets. When the Chofetz Chaim saw this, he immediately cried out to God, "Where is Your justice? For it is written, **'You shall not afflict any widow or orphan. If you afflict him at all, and if he does cry out to Me, I will surely hear his cry; and My anger will be kindled, and I will kill you with the sword'"** (see Exodus 22:22-24). Thirty years later, Dobbie was bit by a rabid dog and died the slow death of rabies, howling like a dog. To this the Chofetz Chaim said, "I now know that God is both true and just." This may be an extreme case, but I believe it illustrates a point well. God takes the welfare of His children very seriously. While God forbid that those who call themselves Christians would actually afflict the helpless, we do have the largely untapped ability to help them.

As Christians, an essential part of our makeup is that we strive to emulate Jesus—to not only grow closer to Him, but to also be like Him. I believe that an important piece of this is justice. One of the prophecies given concerning Jesus states, **"And (God) shall make Him of quick understanding, and His delight shall be in the reverential and obedient fear of the Lord. And He shall not judge by the sight of His eyes, neither decide by the hearing of His ears; but with righteousness and justice shall He judge the poor and decide with fairness for the meek, the poor, and the downtrodden of the earth"** (see Isaiah 11:3-4 AMP). This is an essential element of who Jesus is, so much so that it is given as one of the messianic prophecies by which we are able to identify

Christ. If it is such an essential element of who He is, it should also be an essential element of who we are as the body and bride.

It should be stated here that this is not advocating a social justice gospel. A social justice gospel believes that the primary reason Christ died was to elevate the lowly, create social equality, and to make all people equal. Thus, in the view of a social justice gospel, the primary purpose of the church is to see those things established in this world. This has even led some groups to developing and advocating a Christian communism. While it is evident throughout Scripture that social justice has always been near to God's heart, it is not the gospel. The gospel of Christ is Him crucified in order to bring man into right relationship with God, thus enabling the establishment of His kingdom upon this world for the benefit of the bride, His people. The mission of the church is to preach that gospel to the ends of the earth and work to establish that kingdom. Of this mission, justice is certainly a part, perhaps even an important part, but it is only a part.

Having put justice in its proper place, let us look at the diverse aspects of justice and what that means for us. It has already been stated that an essential aspect of biblical justice is caring for the widow and orphan, helping those who are in need. There is a hurting, dying world out there, and as much as they need to know Jesus, they need real aid as well. However, justice goes beyond just that.

Justice is an essential element of our warfare. Psalm 89:14 states, **"Righteousness and justice are of the foundation of Thy throne."** Without a doubt, we find ourselves in a war between two kingdoms, the kingdom of God and the kingdom of this present darkness. There is nothing more opposite than these two kingdoms. Thus it stands to reason if the foundation of the throne of God is righteousness and justice, then the foundation of the enemy's kingdom would be unrighteousness and injustice. Paul writes, **"For we wrestle not against flesh and blood, but against principalities, against powers, against the rulers of the darkness of this world, against spiritual wickedness in high places"** (**Ephesians 6:12** KJV). I know a little about wrestling, having been a wrestler. I also had the opportunity to train under one of the best wrestlers of all time, Dan Gable. One thing he said always comes to mind when I read this passage. Dan won a gold medal in the 1972 Olympics. He won without ever having an opponent score a point against him. I asked him once how he did it. He said, "Simple. I attacked my opponent's legs; that way he couldn't attack mine." The more we are on the offensive against our enemy, and even attacking the very foundation of his throne, the less he will be able to attack us.

Another aspect of justice is that it is a garment. It is in fact essential clothing in order to enter the Holy of Holies. Exodus 28:29 states, **"So Aaron shall bear the names of the sons of Israel in the breastplate of judgment** (justice) **over his heart, when he goes into** the holy place..." (NKJV). The breastplate of justice is one of eight specific garments the High Priest had to wear into the Holy of Holies. Now we know that the things of the Old Covenant are a type and a sign for the things of the New Covenant. I believe that one of the things that will determine how close we can come to God in worship and our daily lives will depend on how heavily the burden of justice lays upon our hearts.

Justice, true justice, seeks to bring healing. Justice seeks to heal relationships. Jesus tells His followers, **"Moreover, if your brother sins against you, go and tell him his fault between you and him alone. If he hears to you, you have gained your brother. But if he will not hear, take with you one or two more, that by the mouth of two or three witnesses every word may be established"** (Matthew 18:15-16 NKJV). While in the end this formulation may lead to different actions being taken, I believe that it is self-evident that its intention is the prevention of escalating hostilities. Rather, it seeks to heal the relationship between the individuals. Here again the image of God as divine Parent comes into play. Every parent is capable of settling disputes between their children, but what parent would not prefer that their children work it out between themselves?

Godly justice also attempts to restore fallen individuals. **"Brethren, if any person is overtaken in misconduct or sin of any sort, you who are spiritual [who are responsive to and controlled by the Spirit] should** set him right and restore and reinstate him, without any sense of superiority and with all gentleness, keeping an eye on yourself, lest you should be tempted also"(Galatians 6:1 AMP). This is where the justice of God and the justice of the world diverge. The justice system of the world seeks to punish and discipline those found in wrong-doing. However, God's justice system seeks to heal and restore. It calls upon the body of Christ to come around the fallen individual, to stand for him, and to lift him back up.

A distinction that needs to be made here is between the Old Testament and the New Testament. I believe that at the heart of the Old Testament you find this same system; however, at the same time you find numerous punitive measures. Everything from capital punishment to corporal punishment is meted out for various offenses in various sins. By the time of Jesus that system was broken, but that was not the way it was supposed to work.

As I have written before,[30] a person who was repentant was to get no punishment. The whippings and other punishments so often found were only for those who were brazen sinners with no remorse or repentance. It also needs to be noted that the Old Testament contains instructions on running a national government, not just a faith community. What we are speaking of here, and what the New Testament is primarily concerned with,

---

30   See Chapter One, "The Trial of Jesus".

is simply the operation of the faith community. One should not look to the various punishments of the Old Testament as justification for punishing those who are in sin and repentant within our faith communities. It is God's will, and the very reason that Christ died, to restore the repentant individual, not to punish them.

When the body of Christ is willing to stand with a person, and restore and reinstate him, they bestow a tangible grace that takes away shame. I have seen many heartbreaking instances, where because of some failing, whether it be sexual immorality, financial impropriety, drug abuse, or divorce, a person with a true calling from God is excluded from ministry due to the body of Christ's inability to restore such a one.

I will never forget one instance that went the other way. A friend of mine in ministry, who had come out of a drug and gang culture when he became a Christian, slipped back into drug abuse. He went to the leadership of the ministry he was working for and confessed his problem to them. The leadership told him that they were committed to *him*. While they could not condone his actions and would insist that he receive treatment, they were committed to seeing him restored and reinstated. What was so touching to me in this was that instead of hanging his head in shame, he was able to freely admit his shortcomings, simply because he knew he had friends at his back. In truth, we as the body need to remember there is only one unforgivable sin and none of those listed above are it.

In truth, while justice does contain a legal element, it is so much more. In the end, it is bearing a heart-burden for your fellow man, wanting to see each individual treated properly and fairly. This is what true justice is. Into this, I would like to bring one final point of discussion, and that is motive. As a rabbi, I bridge two worlds, the Christian and the religiously-committed Jewish world. As such, I am privy to many conversations and thoughts that those only in the Christian world are not. One of the main criticisms I hear concerning Christian charity and social justice is that it is done with an ulterior motive, to win souls. Please hear what I am about to say in the spirit in which it is intended, as someone who loves the church and only wants to see her shine. It pains me to hear these opinions, but often they are true. Many times the way the church has conducted itself in these things has led the world as a whole to believe that the church really does not care about the people, but only about the number of souls that can be saved.

One instance that struck me was when the MorningStar ZAO water project was first getting started, they did a study of water and wells in Africa. They found that different missionary organizations had dug hundreds of wells, but lacking basic maintenance, they were now inoperable. In the eyes of the world, actions such as these give the church a huge black eye because it seems that the wells were only dug in order to save souls, and once the soul-winning was done, they left the people without continuing support or training. I am not saying preaching the gospel of Christ should not be the highest priority. However, we may want to consider our methods. Perhaps we should do these things because they are the right thing to do and because we emulate Christ when we do them, thus opening doors for the gospel, rather than doing them because they give a platform to preach.

So many organizations that now oppose the church have some social justice issue at their base. These could be our friends, not our enemies. If we take on issues such as poverty, homelessness, women's circumcision, and racial cleansing not because we want to forward an agenda but because it is the right thing to do, we would make a great number of friends and open doors that we never dreamed possible. In the end, justice is a love for people and Christian justice is about being a conduit of God's love for people. With that in mind, it seems only appropriate to end this chapter with some of the greatest words ever written on love: **"Love is patient, love is kind and is not jealous; love does not brag and is not arrogant, does not act unbecomingly; it does not seek its own, is not provoked, does not take into account a wrong suffered, does not rejoice in unrighteousness, but rejoices with the truth; bears all things, believes all things, hopes all things, endures all things. Love never fails"** (see I Corinthians 13:4-8).

CHAPTER NINE

PRACTICAL STEPS: TAKING MARRIAGE BACK

FROM THIS POINT, I HOPE TO LAY OUT several areas and ways in which the body of Christ can extend justice both within her midst and also in the world around her. As the argument was made in the previous chapter, the church is called to be the headlamp for the world, not the tail. We should be lighting the way for the world to follow. No other religion or anti-Christian organization should be outdoing the church in this area. Rather, the church should be miles ahead of any of them, and in truth it is well within the power of the body of Christ to be so.

As the church proceeds toward reclaiming its biblical system of justice, we could expect it to take years or even decades before we have a viable system operating within our churches on all levels. There are many things that we need to have in place. The two most important are God's ordained elders and the trust of the flock. I believe that God has already sent His ordained elders and they already are in our midst. The greatest issues will be proper training and people learning to trust the eldership. Therefore, we should consider looking for very practical steps through which we could implement this system and begin to gain that trust.

One of my martial art instructors once drilled into my head that in any given situation one should neutralize the greatest and most immediate threat first. I believe that the enemy is attempting to undermine the body of Christ on many levels by substituting his foundation of injustice and unrighteousness for the foundation of God's throne which is righteousness and justice. I also believe one of the enemy's greatest attacks is in the area of marriage. A recent study concluded that in the United States, couples are divorcing at a rate of 50 percent (U.S. Census 2002). Sadly, a recent Christian study states that born-again Christians are divorcing at the same rate as non-Christians (Barna 2004). If our marriages are taking casualties at such a high rate, then there can be little doubt that this is an immediate and serious threat to the holiness and righteousness of our body and faith communities. It is also an area in which I believe the church can most easily begin to take steps to counter.

Within Orthodox Judaism, the divorce rate is currently holding somewhere around 3 percent (NCSY et al 2002). This is a stunning difference to be sure. There are various factors which contribute to this lower rate. Courtship customs cannot be disregarded, and for the church to mimic such customs would in fact take many years. However, beyond the initial formation of the relationship, there are many factors which the church could currently institute.

One of the major differences that exists between Christians and Jews is the acceptance of divorce as a very real possibility for the ending of a marriage. Many churches and even some denominations do not view divorce as a valid option and, as a result, fail to plan or prepare for the possibility. Simply, we do not attempt to prevent what we do not believe will happen. For instance, if the moon was to fall from the sky and collide with the earth, it would be absolutely catastrophic; yet, the governments of the earth have no plans for such a contingency because we do not believe that it will ever happen.

Within Judaism, the situation is very different. In Deuteronomy, it says, **"If a man marries a woman who becomes displeasing to him because he finds something indecent about her, and he writes her a certificate of divorce, gives it to her and sends her from his house" (see Deuteronomy 24:1 NIV).** The rabbis have consistently interpreted this verse to mean that a person can divorce a spouse for any reason. However, they also believe that the consistent witness of Scripture brings one to understand that "the Torah wishes to prevent a divorce at all costs," which is derived from the following: **"Another thing you do: You flood the Lord's altar with tears. You weep and wail because he no longer pays attention to your offerings or accepts them with pleasure from your hands. You ask, 'Why?' It is because the LORD is acting as the witness between you and the wife of your youth, because you have broken faith with her, though she is your partner, the wife of your marriage covenant. Has not [the LORD] made them one? In flesh and spirit they are his. And why one? Because he was seeking godly offspring. So guard yourself in your spirit, and do not break faith with the wife of your youth. 'I hate divorce,' says the LORD God of Israel"** **(see Malachi 2:13-16 NIV)**. There are several keys to this, one of which is preventative maintenance.

Once on a flight to Israel, I was seated next to an Israeli Air Force (IAF) aircraft mechanic. As is often the case on long flights with nothing else to do, I began talking to this person, especially about what he does in the IAF. As it turns out, he was a career soldier who absolutely loved everything about his job. He literally went on for hours about maintenance schedules.

At one point, I sarcastically interjected, "whatever happened to, 'if it isn't broke, don't fix it.'" His reply was simple: "That works for cars—if your engine fails, you pull off to the side of the road and wait for the tow truck. However, at 20,000 feet, an engine quitting is not so easy to walk away from." He then elaborated by telling me all of the horrible things which could happen to the aircraft that I was currently sitting in if its mechanics had taken shortcuts. Soon, I was as interested in his subject as he was. I was amazed when he told me that jet engines are often rated for a certain number of operational hours (after which they are known to begin to fail), and so they often change them out long before they hit that magic number.

As it turns out, 34 percent of marriages fail within the first three to four years (Janus & Janus 2004). In other words, most marriages, like aircraft engines, have a predictable breakdown rate, which could possibly be prevented. The key is scheduled maintenance. Within Judaism, the rabbi who marries a couple is responsible for the marital health of the couple—he is the mechanic.

A problem I have noticed in many marriages is that both parties often believe that married life will be easy and problem free. Sadly, in many cases, pastoral premarital counseling does little to dissuade them of this. One instance that comes most immediately to mind is some friends of mine who married each other about eight years ago. At the time, I was involved in a Christian church. I was friends with the lady, who was also my pastor's daughter, and the gentleman was in a small group which I was leading. For Christians, they had a relatively short courtship, just six months, and because I knew them well, I tried to warn them of potential problems in their relationship. From what I knew of each of them, I could see that there were major differences in the ways they handled various situations. I wish I could say that my warnings were heeded; rather, I was accused of jealousy and simply disregarded. They were both Christians and expected their relationship would be a breeze.

Over the years, I drifted away from those two, but I always wondered what became of them. Recently, my wife and I were flipping through the channels on television—I was shocked to see both of them on the *Dr. Phil* show. Their marriage was in shambles; their faith community had not been able to help them. Now they were seeking help on a national television show. I cannot begin to imagine the incredible stress one has to endure to be pushed to that point. However, I am fairly certain that effective, premarital counseling in their case probably could have avoided the things which had become issues in their marriage. For certain, post-marital counseling would have helped as well. We need to take responsibility for the marriages we make—both in the formative stages and in the maintenance.

Preventative maintenance is good, but first we have to know what is going to break. For example, with a Boeing 747, from what I understand, all of them will most likely wear out in the same way, as all of the parts are generally the same. With people, however, each one is unique. Therefore, the problems in each marriage will also be unique. This poses a slight problem that calls for a creative solution. In Judaism, where rabbis are considered responsible for those couples whom they marry, they have made premarital counseling into an art form. Couples must first take classes, and at times, depending on the number of couples engaged within a community, they may take them with other couples. These classes will cover the basics of forming a proper religious home with God at its center, the roles of husband and wife, basics in childrearing, and also applicable scriptural laws concerning purity and intimacy.

Once that phase is completed, the couple will then be scheduled for private counseling sessions in which they make use of extensive questionnaires. One such questionnaire is provided in Appendix A. The point of the questionnaire is to have the couple asking the right questions, and when important issues arise because of them, resolve them before they become major problems for the relationship. The idea from the pastoral perspective is to try to create an environment free from any judgment or fear, where the two can feel free to respond and react to each other, and the pastor acts more like a facilitator.

The pastor's job, however, is more than simply being a facilitator; he also needs to be an active listener. Where he sees contention, he should try to help the couple resolve it, being mindful that many couples, especially as they approach marriage, would rather sweep many of these issues under the rug than deal with them head on. As much as possible, the pastor should try to prevent this. The pastor should also look for areas of future contention. Warning signs would be that issues are avoided or not resolved, when one or both parties respond with contempt to the other's concerns, if one person gets defensive or offensive instead of addressing the partner's complaint, or if their communication styles result in increased conflict instead of resolution. I would suggest, if at all possible and both parties agree, that the pastor record these sessions for personal review as well as future reference. Remember, a pastor is the primary mechanic in the relationship and will need some type of copy of the original diagnostic tests.

An important issue to bear in mind is that every person has issues which are negotiable and those which are non-negotiable. Most relationships have irreconcilable differences, things that the couple do not agree on and may never agree on, but these need not end the relationship as long as the partners are aware of them and are willing to deal with them. If they are not willing to deal with them, but rather they are a constant cause of frustration and conflict, more serious measures may be necessary. This could involve delaying the wedding until these issues are resolved, or even referring the couple to professional counseling.

These things could also be an indicator that the couple is feeling pressure to get married before they are truly ready to make the commitment. This could be for a number of reasons: Their friends may all be getting married, younger siblings could be getting married and they feel embarrassment, or one I have seen too often is a young couple who, because of passion and hormones, have committed some sexual indiscretion and now feel the need to make it right. There are many reasons to get married, but the above are not among them. While I think a pastor should rarely tell a couple that they should not marry, it is within his prerogative to require them to wait until they have these issues resolved.

Oftentimes, pastors or ministers may be faced with marriages that are already in crisis. These may be people who have wandered into our ministries and churches, or they may be couples whom we have married years prior and for whatever reason have not been preventative enough. In these situations, time is of the essence. Usually a couple will not even realize that their relationship is in trouble until it is really in trouble, and then they will usually not seek help until serious damage has been done to the relationship. However, this can be prevented. If we, as ministers, and even friends, have intentional relationships with those around us, we can try to help them both see the problems building and help resolve those problems. Often, if we are observant of those around us we will see problems building long before they ever surface.

From my personal life, I can offer an example of when this was done correctly. At one point, shortly after the death of my father, my wife and I had a fairly major blow-up right inside our church lobby. The pastor who oversaw our premarital counseling witnessed it, and at different times shortly thereafter asked both of us, essentially, if this was a building problem or if it was simply a one-time incident. At the time, we both thought it was just a one-time incident; however, a few days later, it happened again. That pastor's intervention on Sunday made us both get a little introspective with our marriage and talk about what issues were behind this behavior. As it turned out, I was dealing with grief and stress and not confiding any of it in my wife as I should have been. My wife was feeling me withdraw and distance myself from her (as well as others around me), and so she was also feeling increased levels of frustration. Our frustrations were building off of each other until they were beginning to explode. However, because we were able to talk about it, we were able to alleviate the situation. Because someone who is both a friend and a spiritual leader was willing to notice and comment on something out of the ordinary, we were able to work on it and fix it.

Often, we can go a long way in helping those we care about simply by noticing and being willing to confront actions and interactions that are out of the ordinary. If we notice growing levels of hostility or distance between couples we know, these could well be early indicators of serious problems beginning underneath. If we can help those we care about intercept these problems, we may be able to help them keep their marriages from going into serious crisis. Helping marriages in crisis is far beyond the scope of this one chapter, or even the scope of this book, and will need to be elaborated upon in the future.

Unless the pastor or minister is a trained professional, it may at times become necessary to bring one into the situation. Considering that counseling is a means to help couples communicate about their issues, it should not be looked down upon to seek professional help. I would suggest that churches and even ministries, if they deal with different pastoral issues, either bring a person who has been extensively trained in counseling on staff, or develop a relationship with a counselor of likemind to whom they can refer their people.

It is important for a pastor to remember that what these people are confiding to him is confidential information and cannot be divulged. If he then wants to discuss a situation with another person, whether another pastor or a mental health professional, simply for the purpose of consultation or to determine appropriateness of referral, the pastor must take extreme caution to protect the identity of those who have placed their trust in him, or must get the couple's permission to discuss them with each individual from whom they intend to seek advice or outside help.

It is also important to bear in mind, especially when dealing with premarital counseling, that prolonged pastoral or professional counseling may actually lead the couple to decide they are not right for each other and to disengage. I have known several pastors who have tried to prevent this. In a word, *don't!* It is not the pastor's job to make a courtship work! If the couple, through the aid of counseling, decides they need to end their relationship, this may actually be a blessing. It is important to bear in mind that many couples have a very rosy view of their relationship at this point, so if they willingly disengage on their own accord, this has probably saved them the future heartbreak of divorce.

As the church steps forward and begins to take authority in the area of marriage, many of its current concerns will evaporate. Many of the things that the world legislates as far as marriage and divorce, which the church now fights, will prove to be paper tigers set up by the enemy to distract us. For instance, I have spoken with many pastors who have been seriously concerned by the possibility of governmentally sanctioned homosexual marriage. While I am not in support of such a position, like many of my rabbinic friends, I consider it to be a non-issue. In Judaism, we have never honored or recognized a marriage made outside of our own faith community. This, too, is a position I believe would well serve the church. To this point, we have spoken about leadership responsibility in the formation of a relationship. Now it is time to talk about kingdom authority within the area of marriage. In many ways, it is time to take marriage back!

Marriage is a divine ordinance of God. Jesus teaches, **"Haven't you read," he replied, "that at the beginning the Creator 'made them male and female', and said, 'For this reason a man will leave his father and mother and be united to his wife, and the two will become one flesh?' So they are no longer two, but one. Therefore what God has joined together, let man not separate"** (**Matthew 19:4-6** NIV). Quite simply, the world has no right to the things of God; they are solely the domain of the body, the citizens of the kingdom. In Judaism though, when we marry a couple we are in fact, in a small sense, writing Scripture. This is a statement which needs some explaining.

When we marry a couple, an amazing thing takes place. No longer are these two free to seek romantic relationships with other people—that is now a sin. Nor are other people allowed to seek those sorts of relationships with them—this also becomes a sin. Jesus states, **"You have heard that it was said, 'Do not commit adultery.' But I tell you that anyone who looks at a woman lustfully has already committed adultery with her in his heart"** (Matthew 5:27-28 NIV). To put this into context, **"lust"** here is better translated as "desire," and **"woman"** better as "another's wife."

As stated previously, for a single man or woman to look upon a single woman or man with some sexual desire in their hearts is both fine and natural. If it was not this way, people would not get married and propagate the race. However, the moment a man or woman is married, it now becomes a sin for anyone to look on them with desire in their hearts. The difference between unmarried and married is only a matter of minutes and God's ordained people pronouncing them married. However, this short span of time and pronouncement makes the difference between a God-ordained desire and a God-despised sin. This is not power we should allow any secular government to wield over God's people.

In the same way, in Judaism we do not recognize secular divorces. For just as marriage establishes Scripture in a sense, so does divorce abolish it, and this is something we are even more uncomfortable with a secular government doing. However, it is a power which much, if not all, of the church has given over to the world, but we can take it back. To bring this down to a practical level, I want to lay out a suggestion for how a church, ministry, or movement could work to reclaim marriage for the kingdom.

STEP ONE:

Step one will be for pastors and ministers to begin to take serious ownership of the people whom they are going to join together in marriage—both by intense premarital counseling and post-marital maintenance. Love and care coming from the leadership and being demonstrated by real deeds is the foundation upon which the rest will either stand or fall. Along with this level of caring must then come solid teaching on the importance and holiness of marriage, as well as the importance and need of what is yet to come.

STEP TWO:

Step two will be to insist that all couples whom we marry sign a prenuptial binding arbitration agreement that should any problems arise within the marriage, they would be handled solely by the church or their appointed representatives, and if the marriage is irreconcilable that its dissolution also be handled by the church. This is a common part of every Orthodox Jewish wedding. We insist that couples wanting to be married within our ranks sign one of these agreements, thus barring the resolution of their marriage from being in the hands of the world.

STEP THREE:

Step three will be to offer these agreements to those already married within our body or without.

STEP FOUR:

Step four begins to complicate things. At this point, once significant success has been seen with steps one and two, I would suggest that the church begin to cease recognizing marriages not performed under the auspices of the church. This would be most easily accomplished by barring those not married under the auspices of the church from official church membership, just as we would bar those living in any other sin from church membership. I suggest that pastors accommodate those who seek membership in their body by performing a "quickie" ceremony for any already married within the world. (This is regularly done within Judaism to great success.) With this would also come asking all who wanted membership within our body to sign a binding arbitration agreement.

The above four steps are worded rather forcefully; however, they should not be implemented forcefully. All of this should be done slowly and with full consent of the congregation as we explain in love and tenderness both the reasons for the need and how it will only help and better the body in the end. I am convinced beyond a doubt that if we approach this properly our congregations will not only want it, but probably complain that we are going too slowly. I also believe these simple things will begin the removal of some of the greatest shame from the church, as well as open the doors for true justice to be birthed within the church.

STEP FIVE:

There is a fifth and final step, and this is for the church to fight for its rights. Given the level of both the attack the enemy has brought thus far against marriage, and the level of success that the enemy has seen in this arena, he is not going to give up without a fight. We are going to have to meet him head-on in this fight. If we are going to redeem the full holiness of the marital covenant within our bodies, then we are going to have a serious fight on our hands. Even within Jewish circles, it is a constant battle, not just in the spiritual realm, but also in the secular. From the establishment of the Jewish prenuptial agreement in the 1950s, I do not believe that there has been a single decade in which there has not been a legal battle over the issue. It is a challenge that the Jewish community has risen to and proven the equal of every single time, but it has been a fight.

As the body of Christ, I do not believe that we can expect any less of a fight. But now is also the time for warriors to arise—those who are willing to take the fight to the enemy's door. Rabbi Gamaliel, the teacher of the Apostle Paul, once said, "If not now, when? If not me, who?" I believe that this question stands today for the church: If we will not stand for marriage, then who will? If we will not do it now, then when will we ever?

CHAPTER TEN

ACCOUNTABILITY AND RESTORATION

AS I WRITE THIS THERE ARE AT LEAST TWO large and public scandals unfolding in the church in the United States. These are not the first, and sadly they will not be the last. In fact, there is probably a fairly good chance that there are many more than this happening on a smaller scale all around the world. There will be failings by those in leadership as it consists of people who are sinners saved by grace, **"for all have sinned and fall short of the glory of God, being justified as a gift by His grace through the redemption which is in Christ Jesus" (Romans 3:23-24)**. The problem is not so much that as humans our leaders will at times fail. The problem is the unwillingness or inability to stand with and restore those that have fallen.

We must be willing to bring our own errors into the light. Paul states, **"But if we judged ourselves rightly, we would not be judged. But when we are judged, we are disciplined by the Lord so that we will not be condemned along with the world" (I Corinthians 11:31-32)**. Once we judge ourselves and deal with our own errors, the Lord will not need the world to do it. Many of the scandals that have broken and are breaking in the body of Christ could have been avoided if the elders had stood up and taken control of things. This is our future. The church that will welcome Christ back to this world will be one that stands for righteousness, both in her own midst and in the world. Long before we will be given authority to judge the world or the angels, we will have to learn to judge ourselves.

> **I say this to your shame. Is it so, that there is not among you one wise man who will be able to decide between his brethren,**

> **but brother goes to law with brother, and that before unbelievers?**

> **Actually, then, it is already a defeat for you, that you have lawsuits with one another (see I Corinthians 6:5-7).**

To be frank, the shame of the church is being paraded throughout the world. Look at the various leaders of the body of Christ who have made the nightly news because of their failings. Often these people, who are so in need of help, are left to stand on their own. They are treated as lepers whose taint we fear may also infect us. However, Jesus broke bread with and cleansed the lepers, and that is where we as the body and bride also belong. Many seem to fear the ridicule that may come from standing for and with an open sinner. However, the choice is a simple one—we can either bear the titles that the world now applies to the vast majority of the church, such as judgmental or self-righteous, or we can bear the titles that they threw upon our Master, being a drunkard or a glutton, one who keeps company with sinners and deviants. Either way, a Godless world will hurl insults. It would be better if we made our camp with Christ. The world may look down on us for being a harbor for those in trouble and those in need, but at least they will know where to turn in their own time of trouble.

One verse often stated to counter association with the fallen is, **"Do not be deceived: 'Bad company corrupts good morals'" (I Corinthians 15:33)**. I will not dispute the veracity of Scripture, but I will say that I believe the context of passage does not lend itself to what is often given as the interpretation. For spatial reasons, I will not delve into the variant readings of the text both in Greek and Aramaic.[31] Left as is, the verse cannot mean all contact with unbelievers and the fallen. There are two very good biblical reasons for this. First, we are Christians, meaning followers of Christ and His message. While

---

31   There are several Greek manuscripts that have a variant reading. Also the two oldest extant copies of the New Testament are two Aramaic versions of the NT. Aramaic was the language used by first century Israel and much of the Eastern Church even to this day, the Khabourix codex(c 165A.D. the scribe an Eastern Patriarch claims to have copied directly from Paul's codex) and the Peshitta (c 400A.D.). I will not enter into the arguments of Greek or Aramaic supremacy, or delve into the complexities of Bible translation. However, these textual variants offer a possible alternate translation which is, "Be not deceived, evil gossip corrupts proper thinking." While greatly different than the version we are used to hearing, it fits much better with the following verse as it would then read, "Be not deceived evil gossip corrupts proper thinking, come to your senses and do not sin"(I Corinthians 15:33-34 translation my own).

Paul in many ways explains, expounds, and expands the teachings of Christ, he cannot contradict them. Simply, we as Christians are supposed to follow the example set for us by the Master. Jesus was Himself condemned by the religious of His day for having dealings with the less than savory. **"The Pharisees and their scribes began grumbling at His disciples, saying, 'Why do you eat and drink with the tax collectors and sinners?' And Jesus answered and said to them, 'It is not those who are well who need a physician, but those who are sick. I have not come to call the righteous but sinners to repentance'"** (Luke 5:30-32).

In essence, the way of the Master was to be around people who had the most need of Him. The Barna study has stated that 98 percent of Christians have no non-Christian friends within two years of their own conversion. If this was because all of the non-Christian friends were now Christians, there would be no problem—a revival would be taking place. However, it is often because we stop associating with them, the exact opposite of what Christ Himself did. To state it bluntly, the majority of the time those in the most need of Christ are not going to be found at church events. I am not arguing that one's primary community or fellowship should be non-believers; however, they should compose a part.

The second major point against distancing ourselves from the fallen comes from Paul: **"Brethren, even if anyone is caught in any trespass, you who are spiritual, restore such a one in a spirit of gentleness;**

each one looking to yourself, so that you too will not be tempted" (Galatians 6:1). There is an alternate reading in the Khabourix[32] codex which I actually prefer, "My brothers, when a person is overtaken by a fault, you who belong to God recover him with a spirit of meekness, being careful from pride lest you also be overtaken" (translation my own). In either reading, the general message is unchanged. The responsibility of the body of Christ is to the fallen brother. Neither variant, nor any version or translation that I have ever read, has ever said that when a brother falls we should distance ourselves as far from them as possible, though that is often the reaction.

A prime example of this was the Jim Bakker/PTL scandal. While many today may not remember this scandal, at its height it became what was probably one of the greatest sources of shame the body of Christ has known in some time. One minister who called himself a friend of Jim's and offered to help later went on the PTL program and called Jim "a liar, an embezzler, a sexual deviant, and the greatest scab and cancer on the face of Christianity in 2,000 years of church history."

In all honesty, it was not the deeds of Jim Bakker that turned this situation into the scandal that it became. If those in authority in the body of Christ had stepped up and stood by Jim, this never would have turned into such a source of shame for the church. Most likely it would have

---

32   An Aramaic copy of the NT dated around 165A.D.

been little more than an unpleasant footnote in church history. In my opinion, it was the colossal mismanagement of the situation by the leaders and elders in the body of Christ that made this what it was.

This is not to say that the church has fumbled every instance. Most likely the majority of us have never heard of the instances in which things were done right. One such instance that I know of could have, if it had gotten out of hand, easily rivaled the PTL scandal. A very successful ministry in Southern California started a church plant/ mission in West Hollywood. Somehow in the process of things, the person who was chosen to be the senior pastor and leader of this plant was a practicing homosexual and warlock, unbeknownst to the parent ministry. Over a course of a couple of years, the congregation of the plant quickly multiplied, and the senior pastor started appointing additional staff.

Everything seemed to be going quite well, until very disturbing reports started coming back to the parent ministry. They came in to investigate and what they found was indeed horrifying. Open sexual deviance, ritual abuse of children, and things that are best not talked about. The difference between this and the PTL scandal was that the leadership stepped in and stepped up. They took responsibility and dealt with the individuals involved. Some were handed over to the authorities, some, when they turned down a restoration process, were put out of the fellowship, and some are now within a restoration process within the parent ministry. Prompt and proper handling of the situation took what could have easily become a national news event and kept it to a one week local news event during a slow news period.

It may offend some that a sexual deviant would be offered restoration. However, like it or not, God is in the restoration business. From the fall of man it has been God's desire to restore and improve upon the relationship between God and man. Two of the greatest New Testament figures were the products of restoration. Paul, who gave approval to the murder of Stephen (see Acts 7) and was a persecutor of the church, was chosen to write the vast majority of the New Testament. Peter actually fell three recorded times—one recorded in Matthew 16, one recorded in Galatians 2, and the most telling of them all when he actually denied Christ three times (see Luke 22). However, after all of this, Jesus took him back and restored him.

So when they had finished breakfast, Jesus said to Simon Peter, "Simon, son of John, do you love Me more than these?"

He said to Him, "Yes, Lord; You know that I love You." He said to him, "Tend My lambs."

He said to him again a second time, "Simon, son of John, do you love Me?" He said to Him, "Yes, Lord; You know that I love You." He said to him, "Shepherd My sheep."

He said to him the third time, "Simon, son of John, do you love Me?" Peter was grieved because He said to him the third time, "Do you love Me?" And he said to Him, "Lord, You know all things; You know that I love You." Jesus said to him, "Tend My sheep.

"Truly, truly, I say to you, when you were younger, you used to gird yourself and walk wherever you wished; but when you grow old, you will stretch out your hands and someone else will gird you, and bring you where you do not wish to go."

Now this He said, signifying by what kind of death he would glorify God (see John 21:15-19).

Not only did He restore him, but also He granted him the high calling of a martyr's death.

Far too often the body of Christ has thrown the fallen on the garbage heap of life, disqualifying highly-anointed people for momentary lapses in judgment or moral character. While we cannot overlook moral failings, neither can we afford to leave them unrestored. Imagine where the church would now be without the works of Paul and Peter, two of its most foundational fathers. How many others who could have been world-changers never got the chance because of a single moral failing? It is the place of the church to welcome the refuse of the world and refine it into pure gold. We should cast none aside, but welcome all who are willing to submit to Christ and be changed into His image with open arms.

CHAPTER ELEVEN
CONCLUSION

IN CLOSING, I HOPE THAT I HAVE BEEN ABLE to lay the foundation or at least the cornerstone for the reemergence of a Christian justice system. It is my prayer that what I have shared here will open minds and stir hearts and that it will begin deliberations and discussions on how to bring this vital ministry about. I have skimmed through a great wealth of information trying to bring forth only what I believe to be vitally important to the beginning of this restoration. In truth, for every handbreadth I have revealed, I have left a mile concealed.

Literally, there is so much more that needs to be looked into, reevaluated, researched, and discussed. I have left core principles such as finances and tithing completely untouched. Whole areas of practicality have yet to be addressed. The full treatment of this subject within Jewish literature consumes barrels of ink and literally covers hundreds of thousands of pages, spanning thousands of years of thought and development. Like any biblical truth, the full breadth and depth will never be exhaustively plumbed this side of the resurrection.

I have done my best to digest that information, to break it down to its most common denominator and to present it in a format that I hope will foment discussion for years to come. My earnest desire is not to be a lone voice crying in the wilderness, but rather to have others pick up this discussion and carry it further. There is much more to be said and many more books to be written. I hope that this will blossom into something beautiful that will change the body of Christ forever, bringing her closer to her destiny as the bride and benefiting God's children.

My primary reason for presently leaving so much concealed is to leave it up to you, my Christian brethren, to figure things out on your own. My reason for this is simple. If we were to implant a Jewish justice system into the Gentile church, we run a great risk of starting on a downward spiral of Judaizing, even though the intentions are right. It is my hope that with the basics that have been laid out here, the Christian church will be able to establish justice within her midst the way God always intended for them. This is why, I believe, Paul did not impose Jewish judicial training on those he released. A person of Paul's stature, himself the chief student of the greatest rabbi of his generation and one of the greatest of all time, could easily have implanted so much more to the nascent church than the few sparse lines spread through his Epistles. Rather I believe he preferred, guided by the Holy Spirit in his choice, that they be led by the Holy Spirit into all truth and, in the process, forge something uniquely their own.

APPENDIX A

Questions to Answer During Premarital Counseling

1. Of all the people in the world, how did the both of you choose each other?

2. How did you meet? What were your first thoughts? Feelings?

3. What attracted you to each other?

4. What do you value and love about each other?

5. What do you expect to be fulfilling and make you happy in your marriage?

6. Where do you plan to live? Are you both comfortable with this decision?

7. What kind of neighborhood and house do you each want to live in? How much personal space and time alone do you each need?

8. What kind of work do you each intend to have? Who will support the family?

9. What are your individual callings? Are they compatible? How do you plan to use them together?

10. How do you plan to manage your personal finances, such as paying the bills, balancing the checkbook, making investments, and using credit cards? Are you both comfortable with this arrangement?

11. How will housework and child-rearing tasks be divided or accomplished?

12. How much time do you expect to spend together every week, and when do you expect to do this?

13. Where/how do you expect to spend the holidays? How do your respective families feel about these decisions?

14. What do you expect to be challenging in your marriage?

15. What stresses you and how do you deal with stress?

16. What makes you and your partner angry and how do each of you respond when that happens?

17. When you disagree with each other, what happens? How do your disagreements get resolved?

18. How long do you stay upset with each other and what kind of issues lead to those feelings?

19. What do you do when you are feeling upset? How does that affect your partner?

20. Do either of you lose your temper (throw objects or hit things or people) when you are angry?

21. What have been the most difficult times you have experienced so far as a couple, and how did you deal with them?

22. How do you feel about separating from your parents?

23. How do your parents and friends feel about your marrying each other?

24. How do you feel about your in-laws, and how do they feel about you?

25. What kind of relationship do you envision having with your parents, respective families, and old friends after you get married? Are you both comfortable with this?

26. Is there anything you think your partner would like you to change about yourself? How do you feel about that?

27. Are there aspects of your behavior that you think you need to change for the sake of your marriage?

28. Is there anything that you would like to change about your partner?

29. What do you think will change in your relationship after you marry?

30. What do you hope will not change and what do you envision having to do in order to keep those parts of your relationship present?

31. What cultural/socio-economic differences do you have?

32. What do you know about your future spouse's culture and its likely impact on your life?

33. Do you anticipate differences in beliefs and values with regard to how you will relate to one another as husband and wife?

34. How will your cultural differences affect your approach to raising children? Which type of education will you choose for your children? Will your cultural or socio-economic differences affect your relationship to your and each other's parents? How will your differences affect your decisions about spending money?

35. What religious differences do you have, and how do you envision these differences affecting you?

36. How do you anticipate religious values being expressed in your home? Are you both comfortable with this?

37. Have you decided upon a church or denomination to make your own? Are you both comfortable with this?

38. How do you envision supporting yourselves over the next several years?

39. Are there any differences in the way both of you handle money?

40. Do you plan to have credit cards? A checking account? Will it be a joint account? Separate accounts? Are you both comfortable with this?

41. How will you make decisions about spending money?

42. Will you be budgeting? How will the budget be decided upon?

43. If you both received a gift of $5,000, what would each of you choose to do with it?

44. Have you discussed any medical or psychological problems you have that might impact your marriage?

45. Have you been sexually active in the past? How does your partner feel about this? Have you been tested for possible STDs?

46. Do you have any questions or concerns about them?

47. How do you each feel about having children? Do you agree about the general number of children you would like to have and when you would like to start a family?

48. Have you discussed your ideas about disciplining and educating your children?

49. How do you think your fiancé will be as a parent?

Excerpted and adapted from *A Practical Guide to Rabbinic Counseling* by Yisrael N., Ph.d. Levitz and Abraham J., M.D., Twerski 2005.

APPENDIX B

The following is a binding arbitration agreement in the form of a prenuptial agreement used by the Beth Din of America (the judicial arm of the Rabbinical Council of America). My intention, for various reasons, is not to have this copied verbatim, but rather to serve as a demonstrative framework for the body of Christ to develop their own type of binding arbitration agreements and even prenuptial agreements. This one has been contested various times in court and has held up every time.

THE **BETH DIN** OF **AMERICA**
BINDING ARBITRATION AGREEMENT

Instructions for filling out this document may be found on the accompanying sheet. It is important that the instructions be carefully read and followed in completing the form.

THIS AGREEMENT MADE ON THE_____ DAY OF THE MONTH OF _____IN THE YEAR 20__, IN THE CITY/TOWN/VILLAGE OF _____STATE OF _____.

between:

HUSBAND-TO-BE: _____

RESIDING AT: _____

and:

WIFE-TO-BE: _____

RESIDING AT: _____

The parties who intend to be married in the near future, hereby agree as follows:

I.   Should a dispute arise between the parties after they are married, so that they do not live together as husband and wife, they agree to refer their marital dispute to an arbitration panel, namely, The Beth Din of the United States of America, Inc. (currently located at 305 Seventh Ave., New York, NY 10001, tel. 212 807-9042, www.bethdin.org) for a binding decision.

II.   The decision of the Beth Din of America shall be fully enforceable in any court of competent jurisdiction.

III. The parties agree that the Beth Din of America is authorized to decide all issues relating to a get (Jewish divorce) as well as any issues arising from this Agreement or the ketubah and tena'im (Jewish premarital agreements) entered into by the Husband-to-Be and the Wife-to-Be. Each of the parties agrees to appear in person before the Beth Din of America at the demand of the other party.

SECTIONS IV:A & IV:B ARE OPTIONAL

(Unless one of these options is chosen, the Beth Din of America will be without jurisdiction to address matters of general financial and parenting disputes between the parties. For more information, see the instructions.)

IV:A(1). The parties agree that the Beth Din of America is authorized to decide all monetary disputes (including division of property and maintenance) that may arise between them. We choose to have Paragraph IV:A(1) apply to our arbitration agreement.

Signature of Husband-to-Be_____ Signature of Wife-to Be _____

IV:A(2). The parties agree that the Beth Din of America is authorized to decide any monetary disputes (including division of property and maintenance) that may arise between them based on principles of equitable distribution law customarily employed in the United States as found in the Uniform Marriage and Divorce Act. We choose to have Paragraph IV:A(2) apply to our arbitration agreement.

Signature of Husband-to-Be_____ Signature of Wife-to Be _____

IV:A(3). The parties agree that the Beth Din of America is authorized to decide any monetary disputes (including division of

property and maintenance) that may arise between them based on the principles of community property law customarily employed in the United States as found in the Uniform Marriage and Divorce Act. We choose to have Paragraph IV:A(3) apply to our arbitration agreement.

Signature of Husband-to-Be_____ Signature of Wife-to Be _____

IV:B. The parties agree that the Beth Din of America is authorized to decide all disputes, including child custody, child support, and visitation matters, as well as any other disputes that may arise between them. We choose to have Section IV:B apply to our arbitration agreement.

Signature of Husband-to-Be_____ Signature of Wife-to Be _____

1.

Initials

IV:C. The Beth Din of America may consider the respective responsibilities of either or both of the parties for the end of the marriage, as an additional, but not exclusive, factor in determining the distribution of marital property and maintenance, should such a determination be authorized by Section IV:A or Section IV:B.

V. Failure of either party to perform his or her obligations under this Agreement shall make that party liable for all costs awarded by either the Beth Din of America or a court of competent jurisdiction, including reasonable attorney's fees, incurred by one side in order to obtain the other party's performance of the terms of this Agreement.

VI. The decision of the Beth Din of America shall be made in accordance with Jewish law (halakha) or Beth Din ordered settlement in accordance with the principles of Jewish law (peshara krova la-din), except as specifically provided otherwise in this Agreement. The parties waive their right to contest the jurisdiction or procedures of the Beth Din of America or the validity of this Agreement in any other rabbinical court or arbitration forum other than the Beth Din of America. The parties agree to abide by the published Rules and Procedures of the Beth Din of America (which are available at www.bethdin.org, or by calling the Beth Din of America) which are in effect at the time of the arbitration. The Beth Din of America shall follow its rules and procedures, which shall govern this arbitration to the fullest extent permitted by law. Both parties obligate themselves to pay for the services of the Beth Din of America as directed by the Beth Din of America.

VII. The parties agree to appear in person before the Beth Din of America at the demand of the other party, and to cooperate with the adjudication of the Beth Din of America in every way and manner. In the event of the failure of either party to appear before the Beth Din of America upon reasonable notice, the Beth Din of America may issue its decision despite the defaulting party's failure to appear, and may impose costs and other penalties as legally permitted. Furthermore, Husband-to-Be acknowledges that he recites and accepts the following:

> *I hereby now (me'achshav), obligate myself to support my Wife-to-Be from the date that our domestic residence together shall cease for whatever reasons, at the rate of $150 per day (calculated as of the date of our marriage, adjusted annually by the Consumer Price Index–All Urban Consumers, as published by the US Department of Labor, Bureau of Labor Statistics) in lieu of my Jewish law obligation of support so long as the two of us remain married according to Jewish law, even if she has another source of income or earnings. Furthermore, I waive my halakhic rights to my wife's earnings for the period that she is entitled to the above stipulated sum, and I acknowledge, that I shall be deemed to have repeated this waiver at the time of our wedding. I acknowledge that I have effected the above obligation by means of a kinyan (formal Jewish transaction) in an esteemed (chashuv) Beth Din as prescribed by Jewish law.*

However, this support obligation shall terminate if Wife-to-Be refuses to appear upon due notice before the Beth Din of America or in the event that Wife-to-Be fails to abide by the decision or recommendation of the Beth Din of America.

IX. This Agreement may be signed in one or more duplicates, each one of which shall be considered an original.

X. This Agreement constitutes a fully enforceable arbitration agreement. Should any provision of this Agreement be deemed unenforceable, all other surviving provisions shall still be deemed fully enforceable; each and every provision of this Agreement shall be severable from the other. As a matter of Jewish law, the parties agree that to effectuate this agreement in full form and purpose, they accept now (through the Jewish law mechanism of kim li) whatever minority views determined by the Beth Din of America are needed to effectuate the obligations contained in Section VII and the procedures and jurisdictional mandates found in Sections I, II, III and VI of this Agreement.

2.   Initials

Each of the parties acknowledges that he or she has been given the opportunity prior to signing this Agreement to consult with his or her own rabbinic advisor and legal advisor. The obligations and conditions contained herein are executed according to all legal and halachic requirements.

In witness of all the above, the Husband-to-Be and Wife-to-Be have entered into this Agreement.

SIGNATURE OF HUSBAND-TO-BE_____ SIGNATURE OF WIFE-TO-BE _____

WITNESS: _____ WITNESS: _____

WITNESS: _____ WITNESS: _____

–END OF DOCUMENT –

The paragraphs below allow for easy notarization. For further information, see the Instructions.

ACKNOWLEDGMENTS FOR HUSBAND-TO-BE

State of _____ County of_____

On the ___ day of _____ in the year __ before me, the undersigned, personally appeared _____, personally known to me or proved to me on the basis of satisfactory evidence to be the individual whose name is subscribed to within this agreement and acknowledged to me that he executed the same in his capacity, and that by his signature on the arbitration agreement, the individual executed the agreement.

_____

Notary Public

ACKNOWLEDGMENTS FOR WIFE-TO-BE

State of _____ County of_____

On the ___ day of _____ in the year __ before me, the undersigned, personally appeared _____, . personally known to me or proved to me on the basis of satisfactory evidence to be the individual whose name is subscribed to within this agreement and acknowledged to me that he executed the same in his capacity, and that by his signature on the arbitration agreement, the individual executed the agreement.

_____

Notary Public

In New York State, the officiating rabbi is qualified to notarize a prenuptial agreement, and he may use the following form.

For other States, please check local rules and regulations.

State of _____ County of_____
On the ___ day of _____, 200_, before me, the undersigned, a person authorized to solemnize a marriage pursuant to Domestic Relations Law § 11(1), personally appeared _____, personally known to me or proved to me on the basis of satisfactory evidence to be the individual whose name is subscribed to within this agreement and acknowledged to me that he executed the same in his capacity, and that by his signature on the arbitration agreement, the individual executed the agreement.

_____

Officiating Clergy/Rabbi

Address _____

State of _____ County of_____
On the ___ day of _____, 200_, before me, the undersigned, a person authorized to solemnize a marriage pursuant to Domestic Relations Law § 11(1), personally appeared _____, personally known to me or proved to me on the basis of satisfactory evidence to be the individual whose name is subscribed to within this agreement and acknowledged to me that he executed the same in his capacity, and that by his signature on the arbitration agreement, the individual executed the agreement.

_____

Officiating Clergy/Rabbi

Address _____

3.

INSTRUCTIONS

INTRODUCTION. This Agreement is intended to facilitate the timely and proper delivery of a get (Jewish divorce document). When a couple about to be married signs this Agreement they thereby express their concern for each other's happiness, as well as their concern for all couples marrying in accordance with Jewish law. These Tenaim Achronim (premarital agreement) should be discussed, and then signed, as far ahead of the wedding day itself as is practically feasible. Full background materials and explanations can be accessed at www.ocweb.org. While it is preferable that the mesader kiddushin (i.e., supervising rabbi at the wedding) take responsibility for explaining the background for, and then implementing the agreement itself–any other knowledgeable rabbi or individual, or the couple themselves, may coordinate the process. Advice of proper legal counsel on both sides is certainly encouraged.

BINDING CIVIL COURT EFFECT. When properly executed, this Agreement is enforceable as a binding arbitration agreement in the courts of the United States of America, as well as pursuant to Jewish law (halakha). The supervising rabbi should explain this to the parties. This Agreement should only be used when the parties expect to reside in the United States upon marriage. Parties should contact the Beth Din of America to inquire about appropriate forms when they will be residing outside the United States. For those who will reside in the United States, the Beth Din will appoint the proper dayanim (arbitrators) to hear and resolve matters throughout the country.

CHOICE OF OPTIONS. The document has been designed to cover a range of decisions which the Husband-to-Be and Wife-to-Be may make regarding the scope of matters to be submitted for determination to the Beth Din. These alternatives are set forth in Section IV. The Tenaim Achronim will be valid whether or not any of the alternatives are chosen. If none of such alternatives are chosen, the Beth Din will decide matters relating to the get, as well as any issues arising from this Agreement or the ketubah or the tenaim. The Uniform Marriage and Divorce Act Section 307 is a general statement of the principles of equitable distribution or community property proposed as a model law. It is not the law of any particular state. Parties who wish greater certainty as to possible future divisions of property (for example persons with substantial assets at the time of marriage or persons interested in taking advantage of the particular decisions of a state where they will be married) should sign a standard prenuptial agreement with the advice of counsel and incorporate this arbitration agreement by reference. Section IV:A deals with financial matters related to division of marital property. If Section IV:A is chosen the Beth Din will be authorized to decide financial matters related to division of financial property. The Beth Din can decide these financial matters in one of three ways. The couple may choose one, but not more, of those ways. If more than one is chosen, all choices are void. If none of such Paragraphs are selected, the Beth Din of America will not be authorized to resolve any additional monetary disputes between the parties.

Section IV:B deals with matters related to child custody and visitation. If the parties choose to refer matters of child custody and visitation to the Beth Din for resolution, they may do so by signing this Section B. They must, however, understand that secular courts generally retain final jurisdiction over all matters relating to child custody and visitation. Section IV:C deals with the question of whether the Beth Din may take into consideration the respective parties' responsibility for the ending of the marriage when Sections IV:A or IV:B are chosen. Section IV:C only applies if the parties have authorized the Beth Din under Section IV:A or Section IV:B, but then it applies as a matter of course, reflecting normal Beth Din procedure. Thus Section IV:C will apply to all decisions authorized under Section IV, unless the parties strike it out. Striking out Section IV:C, while discouraged by Jewish law, will not render the entire Agreement invalid or ineffective.

WITNESSES. There must be two witnesses to each signature. The same people can witness each signature and sign twice, once under the signature of the Husband-to-Be and once under the signature of the Wife-to-Be, or four witnesses can be used, each signing once. It is preferable that each page of the agreement be initialed by both parties.

NOTARIZATION. It is not always legally required to have this Agreement notarized in order for it to be valid and enforceable. Each couple should discuss this question with their legal advisors. Even if there is no legal requirement for notarization, it is certainly a good idea for it to be notarized; hence a notarization form is included in the document. Notaries can usually be found in banks, legal offices, etc. In NY State, the officiating rabbi can notarize the prenuptial.

ADDITIONAL FORMS. Some couples, for financial or other reasons, sign other prenuptial agreements. In such cases they may find it useful or practical to sign this document and incorporate this arbitration agreement by reference into any additional agreement. Additional forms and other material can be obtained from the offices of the Beth Din of America, or by visiting www.ocweb.org.

SAFEKEEPING OF THIS FORM. Husband-to-Be and Wife-to-Be should keep his or her own copy of this Agreement in a safe place. For additional protection, we strongly advise sending a copy to the Beth Din of America as well, for its confidential files.

FURTHER INFORMATION. Further information regarding this Agreement, or further information concerning the procedures to be followed for resolution of any matters or disputes covered by this Agreement, may be obtained either from the Beth Din of America, or from The Orthodox Caucus, which has disseminated this form Agreement. Background information is available at www.ocweb.org.

The Beth Din of America	The Orthodox Caucus
305 Seventh Ave., Suite 1201, New York, NY 10001	2520 Amsterdam Ave. Office 306
Tel: (212) 807-9042	New York, NY 10033
Fax: (212) 807-9183	Tel: (212) 960-0064
Email: menahel@bethdin.org	Fax: (212) 960-5273
Web: www.bethdin.org	Email: info@ocweb.org
	Web: www.ocweb.org

IN AN EMERGENCY Outside of normal business hours, calls may be made to either Rabbi Yona Reiss, Director of the Beth Din of America, at (917) 584-1337 or Rabbi Michael Broyde, Dayan of the Beth Din of America, at (917) 208-5011.

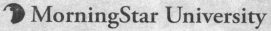